PRAISE FOR *MEDIA INTERVIEW TECHNIQUES*

'Robert Taylor's book is a must for all those who are facing the media. Packed with tried and trusted tactics and dozens of examples from real-life situations, this is an essential read both for newcomers and experienced spokespeople wanting to stay ahead of the game.' **Cathie Burton, Spokesperson, Head of Communication and Media Relations, Organization for Security and Co-operation in Europe**

'I have worked with Robert for many years, delivering courses for diplomats through to management consultants and chief executives of not-for-profits. This book is the culmination of his career as a specialist media trainer. Undertaking a media interview is always challenging but these straightforward and down-to-earth hints and tips make that challenge less daunting, indeed almost something to look forward to. I particularly enjoyed the many anecdotes he includes, many of which are classic examples, which serve to illustrate what you should and what you should not do when tackling a media interview. An entertaining read, combined with sound practical advice, ranging from how to construct a message sandwich through to ideas about posture, breathing and relaxation.' **Caroline Black FCIPR, Managing Director, Caroline Black & Associates**

'Robert Taylor shares a lifetime of experience training spokesmen for media interviews in this one book. It's a treasure trove of information, examples and guidance. Quite simply, if you love or fear giving media interviews you will learn something from Robert's expert advice.' **Vickie Sheriff, former Official Spokesman for the Prime Minister**

'Robert Taylor's book provides a thorough and comprehensive approach to media trai... rt thinking and useful examples, thi... depth knowledge

D1427666

and experience in the world of media and is a must-read for anyone preparing for a media interview.' **Henrietta Mackenzie, Associate Director, Edelman**

'Robert Taylor writes with authority on a subject he knows inside out and with the same easy style you get in his face-to-face workshops. Robert's model works equally for a private sector client, public sector body or a not-for-profit, and has become a core part of our organization's media training programme. I'd certainly encourage any press officer to read *Media Interview Techniques* before prepping their spokesperson for media calls.' **Krysteen Ormond, Public Relations & Media Manager, Falkland Islands Government**

'Robert's coaching and techniques make sure we get the most out of every opportunity to tell "the world" what we do and why it's so important.' **Jonathan Ludford, National Communications Manager, Canal & River Trust**

'This is a genuinely informed and practical guide. Robert starts – and ends – with a reminder that planning for media interaction is an opportunity, rather than a threat, assuming considerable planning and preparation have gone beforehand. All of which is set out with clarity and precision in the chapters in-between. The sections on tone of voice, body language and personal presentation, and messaging, go to the heart of how media performance – good, or bad – can impact a brand. Today's news isn't gone tomorrow: we're reminded that it will be available online and will influence a brand's future for decades. Robert's crystal-clear writing style, along with the exercises ending each chapter, will give any spokesperson or executive the confidence to develop constructive relationships with important influencers across all media channels.' **Donald Johnson, Head of Brand Strategy, National Grid plc**

'Robert has produced a highly authoritative yet very accessible guide for anyone involved in media interviews. Whether you are a first-time interviewee, a corporate communications professional or a training manager, you will find the book's detailed advice and examples reassuring and invaluable. Robert has trained a number of our clients, all of whom have enjoyed and benefitted from the experience. His techniques have prepared them for successful encounters, including interviews on BBC Radio 4's *Today* programme and with *The Sunday Times*' Business section. Robert is a genuine master of his craft.' **Marc Cornelius, Founder and Managing Director, 80:20 Communications**

'Robert Taylor is one of the few trainers in the market who can call upon real-world experience, supporting theory and anecdotal evidence to make his case. Everything in these pages rings true. And he writes well, too . . . This book will be of great interest to students and practitioners.' **Michael Johnson, former editor of *International Management* magazine and director of McGraw-Hill World News**

'Robert Taylor is as thorough as they come and this guide reflects his detailed approach.' **Jessica Dixon, Director, Spider PR**

'"He knows his stuff", one senior official of the Ukrainian government told me after media training with Robert Taylor in Kyiv. I have no doubt he would have been even more eloquent in describing Robert's professionalism, had he read *Media Interview Techniques*. The book is both comprehensive and reader-friendly. A must-read for spokespeople, not to mention anyone striving for excellence in giving interviews.' **Dmytro Kuleba, Ambassador-at-Large for Strategic Communications, Ministry of Foreign Affairs of Ukraine**

'Robert Taylor is an excellent media trainer. Of course, nothing beats having him in person, but this book encapsulates his lessons perfectly and is a very useful reference tool for everyone who wants to present themselves well in front of journalists.' **Charlie Pryor, Director, Leidar**

Media
Interview
Techniques
A complete guide
to media training

Robert Taylor

KoganPage

LONDON PHILADELPHIA NEW DELHI

First published in Great Britain and the United States in 2016 by Kogan Page Limited

2nd Floor, 45 Gee Street
London EC1V 3RS
United Kingdom
www.koganpage.com

1518 Walnut Street, Suite 1100
Philadelphia PA 19102
USA

4737/23 Ansari Road
Daryaganj
New Delhi 110002
India

ISBN   978 0 7494 7472 0
E-ISBN   978 0 7494 7473 7

British Library Cataloguing-in-Publication Data

A CIP record for this book is available from the British Library.

Library of Congress Cataloging-in-Publication Data

CIP data is available.

Library of Congress Control Number 2015032587

Typeset by Amnet
Print production managed by Jellyfish
Printed and bound by CPI Group (UK) Ltd, Croydon, CR0 4YY

CONTENTS

Foreword xi
Acknowledgements xiii

01   Why do a media interview? 1

Have something newsworthy to say! 2
When to decline a media interview 8
Summary 10
Exercises 10

02   Preparing for your interview 11

Basic information you need 12
Anticipate the questions 13
Know your organization's line on sensitive
     corporate issues 19
What's topical in your industry that the journalist might
     ask you about? 20
The role of your PR department 21
Become a great spokesperson 23
Get media trained 24
Summary 26
Exercises 26

03   How to create a resonant message 27

Make your business objective action-oriented 27
No more than three key messages 29
Constructing a "message sandwich" 45
Get to the point . . . 50

Remembering your messages 54
Summary 58
Exercises 58

04   Keeping your cool 61

Too much adrenaline – nervousness 61
Too much adrenaline – anger 72
So should you ever lose your cool? 76
The exceptions 77
Not enough adrenaline – over-confidence 78
What's better: live or recorded? 83
Summary 83
Exercises 83

05   Voice and body language 85

Eye contact 86
Posture 88
Pace of delivery 90
Other aspects of good voice and body language 92
Dress sense 99
Summary 101
Exercises 102

06   The perfect tone of voice 103

A W.I.S.E. tone 103
1 Keeping your delivery as conversational as possible 107
2 Using mind pictures 117
All elements of W.I.S.E. working together 119
Curtailing your curtness 120
Finding the full stop 122
Humour 122
Summary 124
Exercises 124

07 Keeping control of the interview 127

ABC: the bridging technique 127
The helicopter technique 130
The caving technique 131
Avoiding the question – rarely a good idea 131
Repetition of key messages 138
How to get off to a good start in a live broadcast
   interview 140
Handling unfair questions 141
The honest truth 143
Apologizing 145
Getting your company name into a broadcast interview 147
Off the record 149
Summary 150
Exercises 150

08 Winning over sceptical and hostile audiences 151

The spectrum of opinion 151
Bridges of empathy 152
Cooling things down 155
Empathy must be genuine 159
Attentive listening 159
Empathy as a message 161
The "open sandwich" – starting with your example or
   evidence then hitting the key message 162
Insulting, offending and patronizing people 163
Empathy in politics 165
Does empathy work everywhere? 166
Summary 167
Exercises 168

09 Crisis media interviews 169

How *not* to handle a crisis media interview 169
"I'd like my life back" 171

A formula for handling crisis interviews 172
Concern/sympathy 173
Action/explanation 178
Concern and action working together 182
Perspective 183
Being ambushed or "doorstepped" 185
Summary 190
Exercises 190

10   Capitalizing on your interview 193

Analyse what went well and not so well 193
Use social media to ensure your interview is seen, heard or
    read by your target publics 195
And if you don't like something the journalist wrote? 196
Build a strong relationship with the journalist 197
Summary 198
Exercises 198

Bibliography 199
Index 203

FOREWORD

We live in a fast-moving and rapidly changing world. Media is proliferating, and getting your messages across to your stakeholders is more complicated and challenging than it has ever been. Whole generations of consumers are now avoiding traditional television and newspapers, but the importance of giving high-quality and clear interviews is more important – and often more difficult – for all types of spokespeople and organizations.

As anyone who has given an interview knows, the pressure on the interviewee can be very high and even the most experienced spokespeople slip up. Whilst a good interview can help your business or organization achieve its goals, a bad one can be sent around the world in a few minutes and end up online for ever. The opportunities and risks have never been higher.

Robert Taylor's excellent book provides the clearest and most comprehensive manual I have come across, in 25 years in the communications industry, to the whole process of giving interviews to a variety of media. Using examples from his own personal experience coupled with some entertaining and very useful cases from around the world, Robert provides more than just a simple "how to" guide. This book touches on areas that are not only important to the process of giving high-quality interviews, but also many of the key attributes of any good communications campaign. The book neatly covers how to develop accurate and high-impact messaging, how to clearly identify and understand your audiences and how to handle difficult and hostile situations, including crises. Whilst all of these clearly are relevant for media interviews, they are useful skills for anyone who wants to communicate clearly in their professional (and perhaps even personal) lives.

But it is, of course, in the sections where Robert deals with handling interviews that this book shines. From the importance of preparation and thought right through to areas such as voice, posture and techniques for dealing with tough questions, Robert provides readers with an easy-to-follow strategy for maximizing the opportunities and minimizing the risks across the spectrum of interviews – whether live or pre-recorded, press or broadcast, friendly or hostile. Each chapter is peppered with examples from Robert's experience of training thousands of executives from corporations, NGOs, charities and other organizations. The summaries and exercises at the end of every chapter provide an excellent opportunity for readers to apply the techniques and tips that Robert outlines to their own organizations.

I particularly like the way Robert deals with the key challenges around dealing with the emotional side of giving interviews – how to keep your cool in confrontational situations and also how to boost confidence for those people that suffer from nerves. We have all seen those "car crash" interviews where either the interviewee storms off in a huff or they are so crippled with a lack of confidence that you just want it to end. Robert's techniques in this area are particularly strong and useful – as well as being easy to remember.

There are many other highlights in the book and I urge all readers to delve into every single chapter in detail. I would also advise everyone to think about some of the implications contained in the book for their wider communications needs. The book also serves as a useful reference point for people to have at hand as they encounter more and more interview opportunities. I am sure readers will return to it time and time again as they look to improve their techniques and refresh their skills.

What Robert has produced is simply one of those must-read books for anyone who may be involved in giving, organizing and preparing people for interviews as part of their job. Whilst, as Robert says, there is no substitute for a media training session, this book should be on the shelf of anyone who cares about how to give a great interview.

Jim Donaldson is a Senior Partner at FleishmanHillard,
one of the world's largest communications agencies

ACKNOWLEDGEMENTS

Publisher's acknowledgements

Kogan Page and the author gratefully acknowledge the involvement of Gill Pyrah and Michael Johnson, and thank them for their valued reviews of the manuscript for this book.

Author's acknowledgements

My thanks to those who have given their time to help me write this book: Michael Johnson, Gill Pyrah, Jenny Volich, Jasmin Naim, Stephen Taylor, Chris Shevlin, Andrew Tidmarsh, Isabel Russo, Adrienne Thomas, Duncan Sedgwick, Steve Marsh, Jamie Bartlett, Nigel Blackman, Martin Langford, Susan Barty, Edd Withers, Andy Black and Caroline Black.

To my family

Why do a media interview?

Of the thousands of people I've media trained, only one has told me that they positively relished the idea of doing media interviews. All the others have either been neutral about it or, to a lesser or greater degree, nervous. A few have been terrified.

There are plenty of good reasons why people might be nervous about doing media interviews, particularly broadcast ones. You'll be asked a series of questions by someone who is usually a complete stranger and who has a completely different agenda to yours; if you make a mistake or dry up live on air it's likely to be embarrassing; you might be asked questions to which you simply don't know the answer; and if it all goes horribly wrong it will probably be up on the internet somewhere or other and associated with your name for good.

When it's put like that you might wonder how journalists ever get anyone to do an interview at all!

People do media interviews, of course, because they provide an unbeatable opportunity to communicate with and influence the actions of audiences that are important to their organization, such as customers, suppliers, potential recruits, regulators, politicians and so on. Is there an organization anywhere in the world that doesn't need to influence people? I can't think of one. And many organizations seek to influence thousands of people, if not millions.

The media not only has vast reach (CNN and BBC World TV, for example, both reach hundreds of millions of households worldwide), but also targets particular audiences with laser-like accuracy, especially in this digital age. Want to get your message over to people who live in my home town of Tunbridge Wells? Get yourself interviewed by the *Tunbridge Wells Courier*, which almost everyone in the town reads. Or how about if you want to reach decision-makers in the global packaging industry? Do an interview with *Packaging World Magazine*, read by 125,000 packaging professionals across the globe, online and in print.

What's more, people still trust the editorial information they receive through the media more than that same information presented in an advert – and that's despite the reputational hits, especially in Britain, that the media has taken in recent years (the phone-hacking scandal is the most damaging example).

Nielsen's Global Trust in Advertising report 2012, for instance, shows that while 47 per cent of people trust adverts (which, of course, organizations have to pay for), 58 per cent trust the third-party endorsement of editorial content (which, of course, they don't). And it's important to remember that this 58 per cent figure is an average across *all* media. Certain outlets are much more highly trusted than others. For example, according to an analysis by Pew Research Centre (http://www.businessinsider.com/here-are-the-most-and-least -trusted-news-outlets-in-america-2014-10?IR=T) some of the most trusted news outlets in America are the BBC (*dis*trusted by only 7 per cent of people), NPR (9 per cent) and PBS (12 per cent). Among the least trusted is the *Rush Limbaugh Show* (*dis*trusted by 39 per cent).

If you doubt people's trust in the media, in general, to shape their impression of a famous person or organization, think of it like this: almost everyone on the planet has an opinion about President Obama. Some have very strong opinions. But relatively few people have actually met him. So for nearly everyone, their opinion of the world's most powerful person is shaped entirely by what they've seen and read of him through the media.

Have something newsworthy to say!

While it makes sense to aspire to achieve coverage through media interviews, you have to have something to say, something the media are interested in reporting. Clearly not every new thing your organization does is going to be newsworthy. But some things will be, or can be fashioned to become so.

Alfred Harmsworth, founder of the *Daily Mail*, said that a journalist's job was to: "Explain, simplify, clarify". And BBC journalist Andrew Marr has written that journalists: "Take less extraordinary things and fashion them into words that will make them seem like news instead." But don't leave it all to the journalists. You should be busy doing it too, studying the things that your organization does that will spark the interest of the media whose audiences you want to influence. Take good note of the trends and developments in your industry and beyond about which you can offer newsworthy comment. After all, the media is full of features, analyses and reviews, as well as news stories, all of which are supported by comment and opinion from experts.

So what is news?

Definitions of news vary, depending on who you ask. Here are a few from the last 150 years:

- "Sex, sensation, pets, heroism." (Donald Zec, *Daily Mirror* journalist)
- "Crime, love, money and food." (Kennedy Jones, British journalist and newspaper manager)
- "Anything that makes a reader say 'Gee Whiz'!" (Arthur MacEwen, editor of the *San Francisco Examiner*)
- "When a dog bites a man that is not news, but when a man bites a dog that is news." (attribution disputed, but whoever said it first knew what they were taking about)
- "News is what somebody somewhere wants to suppress; all the rest is advertising." (Alfred Harmsworth, 1st Viscount Northcliffe, British publisher)
- "News is what you talk about over a pint." (Alan Powell, editor of the *Sheffield Telegraph*, quoted in *Newspaper Journalism: A practical introduction* by Susan Pape and Sue Featherstone)

Deborah Turness, former editor of ITV News, quoted in *The Broadcast Journalism Handbook*, goes a little further when describing broadcast news, saying: "Every single news item should perform an emotional function. It clarifies something, reassures, explains or shocks. It inspires fear or makes you laugh. It might give you consumer information that makes life easier to live."

For a scientific analysis, we can refer to research carried out in 2001 by British academics Tony Harcup and Deirdre O'Neil. They studied more than 1,000 leading British national newspaper stories, and concluded that they typically fit into a short list of categories, including:

- Surprising and shocking stories;
- Bad-news stories, including tragedies and conflicts of various sorts;
- Good-news stories, such as discoveries and cures for diseases;
- Stories about powerful people and organizations;
- Celebrity stories;
- Various other entertainment stories.

There's no doubt that the biggest news stories – the ones that you remember years later – have many of the attributes Harcup and O'Neil identified. A few years ago I developed a personal list of the top news stories in my lifetime. I decided they should all be single news stories, rather than unfolding dramas such as the fall of the Berlin Wall and the Arab Spring, and as you'll see they reflect the fact that I've spent most of my life in Britain:

1 9/11 terrorist attacks in New York (2001);
2 Death of Princess Diana (1997);
3 7/7 terrorist attacks in London (2007);
4 Resignation of Margaret Thatcher (1990);
5 Space shuttle disaster (1986);
6 Brighton Bomb (1984);
7 Argentina's invasion of the Falklands (1982);

8 Lockerbie bomb (1988);

9 Heysel Stadium tragedy (1985) – 39 football fans were crushed to death;

10 President Obama's inauguration address (2009).

There's plenty of shock, surprise, powerful people and a fair dose of tragedy in that lot.

But what about business stories, such as those covered by the *Financial Times*, *The Economist* and Bloomberg? Do they also exhibit the newsworthy attributes that Harcup and O'Neil identified? Yes they do. On the day I'm writing, these are a selection of headline stories from around the world on the *Financial Times*' website, FT.com:

- "Greece overturns civil service reforms" (This one fits into the on-going bad-news story of Greece's economic problems).
- "Netanyahu struggles to form government" (That's a powerful-person story, if ever I saw one).
- "Bollywood star guilty in hit-and-run case" (Even the FT carries celebrity stories, albeit the focus of the story is about the Indian justice system).

And these are a selection of stories from Bloomberg Business (Bloomberg.com):

- "Chaos is the only sure thing in the UK election" (Bad news).
- "God's new bankers attack Vatican corruption" (This story about Pope Francis' attempts to clean up the Vatican's finances is another powerful-person story).
- "Spain booms, France stagnates as reform diverges" (A mixture of good news and bad news).

In their own way, albeit on a much smaller scale, local and trade-news stories also exhibit the newsworthy attributes that Harcup and O'Neil identified. For example, these are some of the headline news stories in three niche publications from the day I'm writing:

- "Tadano launches latest rough terrain crane" (*Cranes Today* magazine). Tadano is clearly a powerful organization in the world of cranes.

- "Traffic lights back working at major south Devon junction" (*Torquay Herald Express*). This is no doubt a good-news story if you live in or around Torquay.
- "Archbishop signed up for major care conference" (*Care Home Management* magazine). An archbishop obviously qualifies as a celebrity if you work in the care-home sector, and depending on your point of view may be classed as a celebrity in many other sectors too.

Are those stories newsworthy? Of course they are – to the readers of those publications.

So how can we sum up what makes news? My favourite definition, which I believe best encompasses all media and all stories, including analysis, features and reviews is: "**Change** that is **relevant** to the journalist's **audience**".

I've highlighted those three words because of their overarching importance. News has to be immediate and new. If it happened a few days ago it won't interest a morning paper or a TV or radio news bulletin. If it happened last month, it won't interest a weekly. If it happened last year, it won't interest anyone.

And relevance? Well, a new type of roof scaffolding will be utterly irrelevant to most people, but to the readers of *ScaffMag*, the magazine of the scaffolding industry, it'll be fascinating. Likewise, a mugging in the centre of Darlington will be headline news there. But only there. It won't be particularly relevant to people living a few miles up the road in Durham.

Bad things make great news

Gloria Borger, US pundit and journalist, said: "For most folks, no news is good news; for the press, good news is not news." And Marshall McLuhan, Canadian communications theorist, said: "The real news is bad news."

Are they exaggerating? It seems not. BBC Radio 4's *Today Programme* is the most influential current-affairs radio programme in the UK. The great and the good appear on it and listen to it, and it is said to set the nation's agenda each morning. In one of its broadcasts in 2005, according to *The Broadcast Journalism Handbook*, presenter James Naughtie told listeners: "There's news coming in from Russia of a gun battle that's said to be taking place between police and armed men in Nalchik, which is the regional capital of Kabardino-Balkaria. One report from the French news agency, and it's pretty unconfirmed, says armed men entered a school. We don't know any more at the moment, but if it turns out to be something pretty awful, we will let you know."

Naughtie probably didn't mean it to sound quite like that. But his slip of the tongue is revealing. "Something pretty awful" is going to be newsworthy and therefore deserving of our attention. If it was only slightly awful, it wouldn't be.

Bad news makes great news. If you look at my personal list of big news stories above you'll see that six of them are, from any perspective, bad news (1, 2, 3, 5, 6, 8 and 9), and there's also a good argument for number 7 being bad news too – it was after all an act of military aggression that led to a war, even though people in Argentina were dancing in the streets. Number 4 was awful news for some British people and a cause for celebration for others. Only number 10 had, from a British perspective, no bad-news element at all (though I feel sure that many Republicans in the United States might beg to differ).

This preponderance of bad news stories filling our airwaves is another reason why some people are wary of speaking to the media, fearing that the journalist will always look for the negative; that their words will be twisted to mean something they didn't say; and that they will be, somehow or other, stitched up.

Of course those things do happen. More often than we might like. But that's why it's so important to look for the win-win in any news story. Few journalists are interested *only* in getting a bad-news story. What they want is *any* story, the bigger the better, that their audience wants to see, hear or read. Give them that, and they'll be delighted.

For example, take a fire on an oil rig. It's big news. It's also got to be bad news, right? Well, not entirely. The most newsworthy element might be the selfless bravery by the rescue teams or the fact that someone survived against massive odds. The most newsworthy angle depends entirely on your point of view.

Lord Beaverbrook, former proprietor of the *Daily Express*, said that a great news story should "flow like honey", easily absorbed and leaving no unanswered questions. Good news? Bad news? It doesn't matter. All it needs to be is news. Great news.

When to decline a media interview

While there are all sorts of reasons for giving a media interview, there may also be a good reason for declining. Simply, you should decline an interview if there is nothing to be gained by doing it. For example:

1 The broadcast or publication might not by seen, read or heard by the people you want to target.

2 You might feel that you or your organization does not have enough expertise to talk about that particular subject. (For instance, while I'm always delighted to give an interview about media training and media-interview skills, I would decline an interview about some other communications disciplines, such sales techniques or speed-networking skills.)

3 You might decide that the story is an entirely negative or critical one – even if it's not about your organization – and you don't want to be associated with it. For instance, say you represent an IT consultancy and the journalist wants to interview you about an IT project carried out by a major supermarket chain, which went hopelessly wrong. Of course you could do the interview, but that might jeopardize your chances of ever being invited to work with that supermarket chain in the future.

4 Likewise, you might discover or suspect that the journalist is planning to write a negative story about your industry, and wants some choice quotes from industry insiders, which will then be pilloried.

5 You might want to control the message so tightly that you decide to deliver a prepared statement instead. (However, keep in mind that a statement, whether written or spoken, never comes close to matching a proper interactive interview for human and emotional engagement. As John Neffinger and Matthew Kohut point out in their book *Compelling People*, writing something out word for word can create "an emotional fissure between the speaker and the audience. Speaking extemporaneously expresses thoughts and feelings in the moment. Reciting a speech [or a statement] is a totally different activity, more akin to reciting lines in an acting performance. We understand that the speaker endorses the words, but we cannot even be sure he or she wrote them.")

But before you decline an interview too hastily, always consider:

1 Any damage that might be done to you or your organization if you *don't* do the interview. For instance, say your organization, ABC Ltd, manufacturers white goods, but has received criticism from consumers that they are unreliable. If you refuse to do an interview about this with the leading white goods publication, on the grounds that the criticisms are ill-informed and unrepresentative of the majority of your customers, the story that ends up being published might well be much worse than if you had cooperated. It might even include that damning line: "ABC Ltd declined to comment."

2 The fact that the journalist might be important to your organization in the future. Joe Bloggs, a promising and go-getting junior reporter on the *Enfield Gazette*, might be the next industrial correspondent on the *London Evening Standard*. Help him now, and he will be much more inclined to help you in two years' time.

3 The old adage that "no publicity is bad publicity". Of course that's not literally true. Just ask BP in the immediate aftermath of the Deep Water Horizon oil spill in 2010. But for any organization seeking to influence others (ie every organization on the planet), it is worth remembering that you have to publicize what you do somehow, and the media is a great mechanism for doing so. As Oscar Wilde wrote: "There is only one thing in life worse than being talked about, and that is not being talked about."

Summary

1 Media interviews provide an unbeatable opportunity to communicate with and influence the actions of audiences that are important to your organization.

2 The media has vast reach, is targeted and generally trusted.

3 Any interviewee should make sure they have something newsworthy to say.

4 News is: "Change that is relevant to the journalist's audience".

5 Strive to offer the journalist the win-win.

6 If giving a media interview offers no benefit to your organization, decline it . . .

7 . . . while always considering any damage that will be done to your organization if you do so.

Exercises

1 Which audiences does your organization need to influence?

2 Which media are therefore most important to you?

3 What new developments at your organization might be newsworthy?

4 How can you package those developments so that you are able to offer journalists the win-win?

5 What sort of interviews should you or your spokespeople practise during media training?

6 What type of interviews might you decline?

Preparing for your interview

02

Karen Friedman, former US TV reporter and presenter, wrote in *Communications World* (May–June 2005): "As a reporter for more than 20 years I interviewed countless numbers of smart, articulate people who had a lot to say but didn't know how to say it. As a result they missed great opportunities to get their point across and shine in the spotlight . . . Facing any journalist without preparation is bad news. Interviews shape public perception about you, your company and your product."

Well said Karen Friedman. Preparation is indeed a vital ingredient of success in media interviews. Of course it's possible for a spokesperson to "wing it", but that rarely produces the best results. Just as a spokesperson will deliver a better 20-minute speech if they've prepared thoroughly for it, so they will deliver a more effective media interview with plenty of preparation. They will communicate a strong message to their chosen audience and give themselves the best chance of achieving their business objective.

If a media interview is worth doing, it's worth doing well.

But what kind of preparation is most effective? In Chapter 3 we will discuss the single most important element, which is developing your messages, examples and evidence. However, there's plenty more you can do to prepare, and a good starting point is to make sure you have the basic information you need about the interview.

Basic information you need

Nobody should go into an interview, particularly a broadcast interview, without most, if not all, of these details:

1 The name of the publication/broadcast and its audience. Different audiences have different needs and interests, so you must adapt your story and your messages accordingly. Ask yourself whom you really hope to influence? Who can help you achieve your objectives? You'll then be in a position to tailor your messages to your audience's specific requirements.

2 Its style (eg thorough or fast-paced, respectful or aggressive, thoughtful or sensationalist). Again, you'll need to adapt your messages accordingly.

3 The journalist's name and specialist areas. You should look at the journalist's recent work to be clear about the type of story they like to cover, the sort of angle they take and their understanding of the subject of the interview. If the journalist is from a radio or TV station, you should listen to a selection of their broadcasts. If they are a print journalist, you should study a range of their articles. It's all about understanding where the journalist is coming from so that you can pitch your story at the right level, achieving a win for both parties.

4 The subject matter of the interview. Make sure the journalist is as specific about this as possible. If you're an economist and you're going to be interviewed by the *Financial Times*, it's not good enough merely to be told that you will be asked about the global economy. You need something much more specific, such as "recent oil price fluctuations and their effect on international trade".

5 Question areas. A serious journalist won't give you their exact questions in advance, but you should ask them for the broad question areas they wish to address.

6 The type of story the journalist is creating (eg news, feature, opinion etc).

7 The angle the journalist is likely to take. Some journalists may volunteer this if asked, but if not it should become clear by researching other stories they have written.

8 Details of other people from other organizations being interviewed for the story. Again, most journalists will volunteer this information if asked, or at least give an idea of the sort of organizations they will be contacting.

9 Length of interview.

10 Publication/broadcast date.

11 Live or recorded (for broadcast)?

12 Studio audience or callers in (for broadcast)?

Only when you have all this information can you begin to think about the content for your interview.

Anticipate the questions

As mentioned above, a journalist will rarely tell you exactly what questions they are going to ask. After all, an interview is meant to be a spontaneous interaction. But knowing the broad question areas will allow you to start thinking about the specific questions you or your spokesperson are likely to face.

Peter Smudde, assistant professor of public relations at the University of Wisconsin-Whitewater, wrote in *Public Relations Quarterly* (summer 2004): "Since you know who the journalist is, what she/he wants to cover and how, and what the organization is and its audience, you should anticipate what kind of questions the reporter may ask you. Begin with the most basic questions and work up to harder questions in a semi-logical way. Once you have the list of questions, come up with concise and compelling answers to each question that are specific and to the point . . . Take the role of the reporter's audience and ask these questions about your answers: 'So what?' 'Who cares?' and 'What's in it for me?'."

In addition to Smudde's advice it's worth thinking about how you will answer the basic questions (although not always worded in this way) that any journalist is likely to ask about any subject, covering the who, what, when, where, how and why:

- What's new here?
- How big is it?
- When and where is it happening?
- How and why did it happen?
- Whom does it affect?
- What's next?

Of course these won't be the only questions you'll be asked, but they'll certainly give you a good start.

Preparing for hostile questions

Before high-profile media interviews, British government ministers have been known to get every member of their private staff into their office to fire out in quick succession the most challenging and aggressive questions they can think of on the interview topic. That's a great way to prepare, because you don't want the live interview to be the first time you face a challenging question. And although you might not be able to predict *every* question a journalist will ask, with enough preparation and thought you should be able to predict nine out of 10.

We don't have to look too far to see the danger of not preparing thoroughly enough, and taking the journalist's questions for granted. For example, in February 2011, Francis Maude, a British government minister, was interviewed on BBC Radio 4 by the respected broadcaster Eddie Mair. The interview concerned the government's drive to encourage people up and down the UK to volunteer to work on various social programmes, thereby helping to make their local communities better and stronger. This was a key plank of government policy at the time.

The interview started with Maude saying how important it was for people not just to pay their taxes, but to help out their community in a variety of other ways. But what he obviously hadn't predicted – though with a little preparation and thought he surely could have done – was discussion of what volunteering *he personally did*. This is how the interview then went:

Mair: What volunteering do you do?

Maude: I do . . . golly, what do I do . . . erm . . . I do a whole load of things. I'm involved with my local church. Um, gosh, that's a really unfair question cold. But actually the point is . . .

Mair: Well given the fact that we're talking about volunteering and how important it is you might have been able to tell me, because in your manifesto it says 'Our ambition is for every adult in the country to be a member of an active neighbourhood group'.

Maude: Um, well I'm involved in things in my local community. I mean MPs spend their time involved with voluntary groups, erm . . .

Mair: But that's part of your job isn't it? You get paid for that. What else do you do?

Maude: We get . . . we do it seven days a week, kind of thing. I do various things. It's a great question to drop on me, and if I'd had time to think about it . . . My point actually is that most people are doing things in their lives that you could define as volunteering, with a capital V, but which are actually doing things which support their neighbourhood, support their neighbours, and being an active citizen in an active community.

(To hear this amusing exchange for yourself, Google "Francis Maude Eddie Mair".)

We can give Maude full marks for keeping his nerve when he was clearly embarrassed and struggling to think of something to say. And at least he made a good attempt to bridge (see Chapter 7) into his key message. But should he have been struggling? With more support and better advice he might have predicted that an experienced interviewer like Eddie Mair would ask exactly that question. Maude described the question in the interview first as "unfair" then as "great". But surely it was a fairly *obvious* question, and one that he could have predicted and prepared for, had he received appropriate advice.

Maude is far from being the only politician who has failed to predict the obvious, if dangerous, question. In fact he's in excellent company. In his autobiography, *A Journey*, Tony Blair writes: "One rule about giving interviews: never do it without knowing the answer to the obvious question. Sounds simple, but it's amazing how many times even the seasoned pro can walk in full of thoughts, full of great things to say, concentrating hard on what they want the story to be, without ever focusing on the answer to the one question they are bound to be asked."

Blair goes on to describe how, towards the end of his time as prime minister, he gave an interview to *The Times* in which he was asked the obvious but highly sensitive question: "Are you prepared to set a date for leaving?". His ill-thought-through answer was "No I'm not setting a date", which led to the headline "Blair defies his party over departure date". This in turn led to another damaging battle with his eventual successor Gordon Brown, making Blair's departure from Downing Street rather messier and less dignified than it ought to have been.

As Blair admits, with the benefit of hindsight, he should have given much more thought before the interview about how he was going to address that obvious, innocuous-sounding enquiry.

So, a key part of preparation for any media interview is to try to predict the most dangerous, challenging or hostile questions that a journalist will ask (especially the obvious ones!) and then decide how you're going to answer them. Hoping and praying that a killer question won't come up isn't good enough. What happens if it does?

General knowledge questions

When George W Bush was running for president in 1999, he quickly discovered that journalists are quite prepared to humiliate politicians live on TV so long as it provides a good story.

Interviewed by Andy Hiller on WHDH-TV, the NBC affiliate in Boston, Bush suddenly found himself being quizzed on his knowledge of foreign leaders, which was fair enough since were he to be successful he would become leader of the free world. Hiller asked him the names of the leaders of Chechnya, Taiwan, India and Pakistan, all countries in the news at the time, and showed no mercy as Bush struggled to answer. In fact, the future president got only one out of four questions right. This is how the interview went:

Hiller: Can you name the president of Chechnya?

Bush: No, can you?

Hiller: Can you name the president of Taiwan?

Bush: Yeah, Lee [meaning Lee Teng-hui]

Hiller: Can you name the general who is in charge of Pakistan?

Bush: Wait, wait, is this 50 questions?

Hiller: No, it's four questions of four leaders in four hot spots.

Bush: The new Pakistani general, he's just been elected – not elected, this guy took over office. It appears this guy is going to bring stability to the country and I think that's good news for the sub-continent.

Hiller: Can you name him?

Bush: General. I can name the general. General . . .

Hiller: And the prime minister of India?

Bush: The new prime minister of India is – no.

Asking a politician general knowledge questions live on air is a simple enough journalistic device, and it's a great way to get a story. So it's no surprise that the British media are at it too. In 2001, Richard Caborn MP had just been appointed Minister for Sport when sports journalist Clare Balding decided to find out how much of a sports fan the new minister really was. In a live BBC radio interview she asked him a few relatively straightforward questions that any sports fan would readily be able to answer, such as the name of the British Lions rugby captain, the name of the England cricket coach, three jockeys riding at Royal Ascot that week and three European golfers playing in the US Open (Caborn claimed to be a golf enthusiast).

Embarrassingly, Caborn didn't know the answers to any of these questions, and it got his tenure as Minister of Sport off to a particularly shaky start. He remained in the post until 2007, and was involved in a huge number of projects. But ask sports fans what they remember him for now and, if they remember him at all, they'll say the Clare Balding interview.

For Bush, Caborn and the many other politicians who have been caught out in this way, their interviews were embarrassing and undermining. But what could they have done differently? The easy answer is that Bush and Caborn should simply have made sure they were better informed. After all, the questions they were asked weren't *that* obscure.

However, being well informed takes work. Tony Blair gives good advice about this in his autobiography when he writes about his efforts to prepare for media interviews in the weeks before a general election. The British media is fond of portraying politicians as out of touch with the concerns that affect ordinary people, so Blair took care to ensure that he knew the basics of home economics. He writes: "Before the rounds of interviews anywhere near election time, I would have to go through a list of the price of everyday things like a pint of milk, a pound of butter, a shoulder of lamb. Bread used to produce lengthy debate about which type of loaf, white or brown, nothing too wholemeal, nothing too unhealthy, all of it done in the belief that if I knew such a fact, it would mean I might be going down to the shop near Downing Street (not that there was one) and collecting the groceries, which of course I wasn't."

What Blair demonstrates here is that the best media interviewees (and he was certainly one) only become so good through hard work and preparation. And if a prime minister can make time to prepare for nasty questions that just might be asked in a media interview, then surely most spokespeople on behalf of most organizations can do so too.

That said, Blair's approach is not foolproof, because you can never prepare for every general knowledge question that a journalist just might decide to ask. Sure, he might know the price of a pint of milk and a loaf of bread, but what if the journalist asked him about a lamb chop or a packet of bacon?

So here's another way you can tackle general knowledge questions. Don't answer the first question – even if you know the right answer – because whether you are right or wrong you will just invite more. Follow the lead of one of Blair's successors as prime minister, David Cameron. In February 2015 Cameron launched what he called a "war on mediocrity" in educational standards, announcing at a press conference the target that by the age of 12 children should know their multiplication tables. The temptation for journalists was understandably huge, and a reporter from Channel 5 News raised his hand and asked the prime minister: "What's nine times eight?".

I'm sure Cameron knew the answer (he did get a first-class degree in economics from Oxford), but he replied: "I do times tables only in the car with my children on the way to school. And I'm going to stick to that, just in case I get one wrong on your excellent television programme."

Was Cameron dodging the question? No, he was addressing it (see Chapter 7 on "Keeping control of the interview"). He knew that if he answered one question, correctly or not, he might be asked more difficult ones until, inevitably, he would get one wrong. And guess which one would be shown on the evening news? So he politely declined to answer the journalist's question. But crucially he told the journalist why.

Know your organization's line on sensitive corporate issues

You or your spokesperson should expect to be asked any topical question about your organization and its activities, even if it has nothing to do with the subject of the interview. For example, say you represent an IT consultancy, and you've agreed to do a video podcast interview with an IT publication on the subject of data security. Then on the morning of the interview, your company releases its annual financial results, and reports a 10 per cent drop in revenues on the previous year. Will the journalist ask you a question about that? Very possibly. So you need to be ready to answer.

For some questions, your PR department will have "the line" they wish spokespeople to take. In fact, most big organizations maintain a comprehensive corporate question-and-answer document, and a spokesperson should make it their business to be as familiar with it as possible. Otherwise you'll be faced, live in the interview, with a difficult conundrum. Do you answer the question based on your own knowledge and opinion? Do you say you don't know? Do you guess what your PR department might want you to say? Do you say "no comment" (a very bad idea!)?

If you do deliver the approved answer to a particular question, make sure you agree with the PR department beforehand that you may deliver the answer in your own words rather than sticking rigidly to the corporate script. As Barbara Gibson, president of SpokesComm, a media spokesperson development consultancy, wrote in *Communications World* (May–June 2008): "When people deliver words that are not their own, there is a perceptible difference in the way they deliver them. It seems that scripted 'key messages' and reliance on written Q&A documents for interviews tend to have a negative impact on credibility, as rated both by journalists and PR assessors on spokesperson assessments . . . the results I've seen lead me to believe that most spokespeople will be perceived as more open and honest when speaking in their own voice and style rather than delivering scripted messages."

So check this with the PR department, and possibly the legal department (you might have a bit of a fight on your hands there) before the interview. Make sure that they are happy for you to deliver the approved message *in your own words*.

For example, say your company is involved in a legal dispute about compliance with employment regulations. The corporate message might be: "Our company is currently involved in legal proceedings and we cannot release information on this subject until these proceedings are concluded."

But live in the interview, you could give the sense of that message without sticking to the exact wording. So you might say: "There's a court case going on at the moment, and so I can't give you the details you're asking for. But I can tell you that we will communicate fully with the media as soon as we are legally able to do so."

What's topical in your industry that the journalist might ask you about?

Just as a journalist might ask you a topical question about your organization, even if it has nothing to do with the subject of the interview, so they might ask you a topical question about your industry.

Suppose you represent a manufacturing company, and you've agreed to do an interview with a local radio reporter on the prospects for manufacturing in your region. Then the day before the interview, the government announces subsidies for manufacturers to encourage them to invest in your area. It would look very odd and highly unimpressive if you weren't ready to answer questions about the government's initiative.

Again, you need to be careful. Some companies have a policy that their spokespeople should not comment on competitors or industry affairs. Others have a policy that they will comment, but never be critical. It is vital that the spokesperson understands the policy and knows what they can and can't comment on (but see Chapter 7 on how to avoid the specific phrase "No comment").

The role of your PR department

PR people have a vital role to play in media interviews in support of the spokesperson. As well as researching all the information above, and helping the spokesperson prepare their key messages and supporting proof points (see Chapter 3), the PR department should also:

- Ensure that pre-interview questions and requests from the journalist are dealt with efficiently and swiftly.
- Suggest question areas to the journalist based on the spokesperson's knowledge and expertise.
- Seek permission from the journalist to record the interview themselves.
- Ensure that the journalist knows how to refer to the organization and the job title of the spokesperson.
- Do practice interviews with the spokesperson, especially for broadcast interviews, making them as realistic as possible and as tough, if not tougher, than the real thing is likely to be.

Many organizations require a PR representative to be present during any kind of media interview, print or broadcast. This is sensible practice. In print interviews, the PR person can, within reason, take part themselves. For example, the spokesperson can check facts with the PR person, the line to take on a sensitive topic or a particular piece of information the journalist asks for. The PR person may also prompt the spokesperson to deliver a particular message, or may remind them of a specific example or piece of evidence.

Michael Johnson, who was Moscow correspondent of the Associated Press before embarking on a distinguished career in PR, writes: "If the interviewee accidentally departs from the message in a damaging way, it is crucial to intervene before it goes further. In one case at the London-based international satellite communications company ICO my spokesperson, a marketing man, boasted to a group of 10 journalists that a new partner-company knew how to throw its weight around with Washington regulators, saying. 'When these guys say jump, the bureaucrats in Washington want to know how high.' As head of communications I recognized the consequences and tried to signal to the marketing man to hold his tongue. Finally, I had to jump up from my chair, grab the marketing man by the shoulders and suggest moving on to another topic. The next week, the marketing man took a course in media training."

In TV interviews your PR representative has another equally valuable role to play. If a TV crew sets up for filming in your office, or in any other non-studio location, it's the job of the PR person to ensure that the shot is as helpful to your organization as possible. What's in the background? How does the shot look? These matters aren't just the prerogative of the producers. Your PR representative should have a view too.

In his book *Lessons from the Top*, the BBC's Gavin Esler describes an interview he conducted in 2010 with the president of Pakistan, Asif Ali Zardari, and the way in which "an efficient leader's staff will manipulate events for the leader's benefit". Esler writes: "A Zardari aide suggested that the cameraman move the Pakistani flag so that the camera could see the white star more clearly on the green background. Good idea. The cameraman agreed. It looked better. Then, five minutes before we were to begin, another aide brought in two photographs and placed them behind the president's chair. One was of Muhammed Ali Jinnah, the founder of Pakistan. The other was of Benazir Bhutto, President Zardari's assassinated wife. This is called 'dressing the set'. It is not primarily about aesthetics, although bunches of flowers and pleasant lighting can be important parts of any interview. For a politician, it is an important storytelling procedure."

Can a spokesperson's PR aide always dominate a production team in this way? Of course not. (Esler and his team no doubt felt honoured to have the opportunity to interview a head of state, so may have been a little more willing than they would normally be to tolerate major interference.) But nor should they roll over and accept what the production team dictates. The spokesperson's PR team should have a view about how the spokesperson is filmed, and shouldn't be afraid of expressing it, even if it makes them a little unpopular with the TV crew.

Become a great spokesperson

In the March 2009 edition of *Tactics* magazine, communications expert Susan Sommers listed all the qualities the perfect spokesperson should have. These included:

- Being an expert in their field;
- Being available for speaking engagements and media interviews;
- Being well spoken, a good writer and a good storyteller;
- Able to communicate complex thoughts and ideas simply and clearly;
- Able to provide openness and transparency;
- Being respected by the executive team and able to lead in a crisis;
- Able to develop relationships with specific media representatives that will enhance trust;
- Being aware of what is being said about him or her and the organization or company;
- Being certain about what they would like the media to say about their organization;
- Able to create key messages geared to the needs of the media.

That's a pretty specific and demanding list of attributes. But the best spokespeople do indeed exhibit most if not all of them. And this is how they get there:

1 Media training (see below). It's just like learning to drive. The techniques for successful media interviews need to be learned.

2 Taking it seriously. Outstanding spokespeople consider media interviews to be a vital part of their role. They never wing it. They prepare thoroughly for every interview.

3 Practising. The more demanding the interview the more important it is to do practice interviews, if necessary in front of a camera.

4 Making it their business to be well informed about everything a journalist might ask them.

5 Learning from what went well and not so well (we discuss this more in Chapter 10).

Get media trained

It should go without saying that an organization should get its spokespeople media trained. Journalists conduct interviews day in day out, so if your spokespeople have never had any training or practice they'll immediately be at a big disadvantage, just as someone who has never learned to cook will probably make a hash of preparing a meal for a dinner party.

Not only does media training prepare your spokespeople for every type of media interview, from the softest to the toughest, but just as importantly it stress-tests your messages for *all* types of communication, written and spoken. There have been many times that organizations have changed or adapted their messages about products, services or the organization as a whole after a media training session. There's nothing like the heat of a simulated interview to help you work out if your messages will stand up to scrutiny.

Media training is not just about showing spokespeople how to handle nasty questions or look good on camera. It is about giving them the tools and confidence to *maximize the opportunity* that media interviews present, and helping their organization achieve its objectives.

So the media trainer you select should be reputable and experienced with a track record of success (ask to speak to one or two of their clients to get the full picture). And "reputable" and "experienced" does not just mean anyone who happens to be a journalist and who wants to do a bit of media training to supplement their income. While some journalists make great trainers, there is no direct correlation, especially if they only conduct a handful of training sessions a year.

The most effective media training sessions are for no more than three trainees, offering each one the chance to do three practice interviews, which should be filmed (even the non-broadcast interviews). These practice exercises should replicate the kind of interviews that the trainees will be expected to do for real, in terms of subject matter, style and format. The training should concentrate on two main areas: what to say and how to say it, and it should offer a handful of lessons that spokespeople can understand and put into practice. A huge list of key lessons and techniques might sound impressive but in practice will be impossible to remember and act upon in the heat of a real interview.

Do journalists want you to be media trained?

Journalists certainly don't want spokespeople to be *badly* media trained, which can result in dodged questions and robotic recitals of prepared soundbites (amazingly some interviewees seem to have been persuaded that's a good idea – see Chapter 7).

But journalists should welcome someone who has been *well* trained, because that interviewee will go out of their way to offer them a good newsworthy story – ie one that is properly targeted, relevant to the subject of the interview, with good colourful examples and evidence that appeal to anyone watching, listening or reading.

The US publisher Joseph Pulitzer advised journalists to: "Put it before them briefly so they will read it, clearly so they will appreciate it, picturesquely so they will remember it and, above all, accurately so they will be guided by its light."

Exactly the same advice applies to company spokespeople, and if they can meet Pulitzer's requirements the journalist won't care less whether they've been media trained or not.

Summary

1 Make sure you have the basic information about the interview, such as the journalist's audience (readers, viewers and listeners), the journalist's style and intended question areas.

2 Anticipate all the questions, especially hostile ones, that the journalist is likely to ask.

3 Make sure you know your organization's line on sensitive corporate topics.

4 Think about topical questions regarding your industry that the journalist might ask.

5 For TV interviews, work with your PR aide to negotiate the best setting with the camera crew.

6 Get media trained.

Exercises

Consider the sort of media interview that a spokesperson from your organization might conduct.

1 What sort of questions will a journalist typically ask?

2 Will there be any searching or aggressive questions?

3 What sort of subjects should be covered in your corporate question-and-answer document?

4 How might your spokesperson safely adapt the wording of approved answers to suit their own style of delivery?

5 Are there any topical questions about your industry that a journalist might ask?

How to create a resonant message

03

In this chapter, we look at the techniques involved in creating strong, meaningful content for a media interview.

Communications experts, including media trainers, often talk about developing "key messages", by which they simply mean the most important points you want to communicate. That sounds easy, but the unique demands of a media interview, and the fact that all journalists want "a story", mean that media messages, with supporting proof points, usually require plenty of thought and preparation.

Make your business objective action-oriented

You, or your spokesperson, have agreed to do an interview with a journalist. How do you develop your content? A good starting point is simply to ask yourself why you are doing the interview and what's in it for your organization. In other words, work out your business objective.

It is best to steer clear of objectives such as "raising awareness", "building understanding" or "enhancing knowledge", because these objectives tend to lead to wishy-washy, imprecise messages. Also, awareness, understanding and knowledge, in themselves, don't lead to change. Only actions do that. So, try and boil down your objective to an action that you want the audience to take. For example, you might want them to:

- Come to your event;
- Sign up for your newsletters;
- Buy your products;
- Vote for you;
- Follow you on Twitter;
- Sign a petition;
- Write to their political representative in support of your position;
- Apply for a job at your organization;
- Tell their family, friends and colleagues that they support your cause.

All these are actions that you can inspire the audience to take as a result of your interview. They therefore make good business objectives, and that in turn leads to strong messages.

Your business objective is for you, and only you, to know. You don't need to tell the journalist what it is, and in most cases you won't want to, so you can make it ambitious. Think to yourself: what is the very best result, in an ideal world, that could come from this interview? If, for example, you're representing a company that makes software programs for businesses, then an ambitious objective might be for 20 IT directors of prospect companies to ring you up and request a meeting to discuss your services. For a commercial business there is no shame in your business objective being focused on sales of your products or services. The media interview is, after all, an important part of the marketing mix.

If you're finding it hard to look beyond raising awareness of your campaign, product or service, then ask yourself what action, ideally, you'd like the audience to take once you have made them aware of it. And if you're really struggling, just make it your objective that everyone who sees, hears or reads about the interview should tell at least one other person about your campaign, product or service. That, at least, is an action that members of the audience can take.

Written communications expert Chris Shevlin advises his clients to keep in mind the possibility that their desired action might be a negative one. By that he means that their purpose might be to stop the audience doing something that they might otherwise do – something unhelpful to their organization.

That's sound advice, and it applies to media interviews every bit as much. Say you represent a manufacturing company and you or your spokesperson is being interviewed about a factory you intend to build. Many local people might be against the idea because they believe that the factory is bound to cause traffic congestion and noise pollution, and they are preparing to start a petition against the development. In that case your objective for the interview might be to persuade people *not* to sign the petition, by emphasizing the job opportunities of the new factory and by demonstrating your company's commitment to community relations and to keeping noise pollution to a minimum.

No more than three key messages

Once you've decided upon your business objective, you're in a position to select your key messages. You should attempt to communicate no more than three key messages and, depending on the length of the interview, you might decide to communicate just two, or possibly just one. But no more than three, even if you expect your interview to last half an hour.

Why so few? Well, to start with, it's difficult for the spokesperson to remember more than three. That might sound far-fetched, but in the heat of a live interview it's all too easy to forget what you planned to say. In an article in *Tactics* magazine (2003), Tripp Frohlichstein, a US-based media trainer, wrote that he recommends interviewees use just one core message, which he calls "the home base", with sub messages and proof points flowing from it.

But even more important is the audience – the readers, viewers or listeners. They simply won't remember and act on more than a few things you say. A study in 2008 by University of Missouri-Columbia psychologist Nelson Cowan bears this out, showing that the average person is only able to hold three or four new things in mind at once. I see this all the time during my training courses around the world. I conduct an interview with a delegate in front of the other trainees. We all then see that interview played back on video, so everyone in the room has had two chances to see it. Ten minutes later, I might ask what people remember from the interview they've just seen twice. Nobody ever remembers more than three core points.

This applies to even the most high-profile interviews. You could watch the president of the United States doing a live TV interview about the state of the global economy. Later that day, you and all the other viewers will only remember two or possibly three key top-line points that the president made.

So, knowing that your audience won't remember or act upon more than two or three things you say, limit yourself to two or three key messages that you want to make in that interview that will help you achieve your business objective. For example, say you represent a university that is hoping to attract the best students to study humanities. Your three key messages might be:

- We have the best teachers in the country;
- Our courses include work placements overseas;
- Nearly all our graduates get jobs within six months.

Or perhaps you represent a hotel chain. You might have one over-arching message, such as:

- We're striving to offer the best service in the world;

Followed by two sub-messages:

- We offer the best to the business market;
- We offer the best to the tourist market.

Or imagine you represent a technology company that's just launched a new application for smartphones. Your overarching message might be the announcement itself:

- We're launching Asia's most advanced maps app for smartphones;

Followed by two sub-messages:

- They are more user-friendly than any others on the market;
- We've tailored the app to the requirements of Asian users.

Developing such messages might sound simple. However, there is another party to consider here. The journalist. They couldn't care less about your business objective, even if they knew it or suspected what it was. They don't care whether people come to your event, buy your products or follow you on Twitter. All that they mind about is the story – so they want content from the interviewee that interests the audience, makes them sit up and take notice, and encourages them to come back for more. That's all that interests them, and quite rightly too. After all, their ability to create strong, newsworthy stories is what we all pay them (or their advertisers) for when we buy newspapers, visit websites, watch TV programmes or listen to radio broadcasts. It is entirely proper that they should focus on what interests and is relevant to us, their customers.

So when a journalist listens to your key messages, what your business objective is might not even enter their mind. Knowing that they need a story, all the journalist is thinking about upon hearing your key message is this:

1 Does it pass my "So what?" test?

And, if so:

2 Give me the proof.

The "So what?" test

This is when the journalist asks himself or herself if the message matters to their audience. A message doesn't have to be life-changing to matter. But it has to be as many of these as possible:

- Inspiring;
- Interesting;
- Unusual;
- Surprising;

- Informative;
- Educational;
- Entertaining;
- Relevant;
- Topical.

That's how a journalist will judge your message, on behalf of the audience. If your message can't measure up against at least a couple of those items, then the journalist simply won't be interested in hearing about it.

Of course you need to know the journalist's audience to know what matters to them. What interests the readers of the *Financial Times* might well be rather different from what interests the readers of *The Sydney Morning Herald*. Different audiences have different needs, and you must tailor your messages accordingly.

Finding a message that allows you to achieve your business objective *and* answer the journalist's "So what?" is sometimes challenging. Imagine you represent a car dealership, and you (or your spokesperson) are being interviewed about a community bike ride you are sponsoring in aid of a local children's hospice. Your business objective might well be to get more customers through the door of your dealership. But if you went into your interview with three key messages about the great service your company offers, the journalist would quickly lose interest – because what matters to the audience is the bike ride (When is it? How do you get involved? Do you need to be super-fit to take part?) and the hospice (How many children are there? How much money are you aiming to raise? How will the hospice use the money?). The services that your dealership offers are irrelevant to the subject at hand, so your messages will have to focus on the bike ride and the hospice. In this case, you might well have to be satisfied with your company name being associated with a good cause.

Or imagine you represent a company that designs maths textbooks for schools, and you're doing an interview about trends in maths teaching. Your business objective might be to sell more textbooks, but the journalist wants to interview you about the latest approaches to teaching. If you went into the interview with three key messages about how your textbooks are better than your competitors', the journalist would quickly think, "Hey! That's not what I'm interviewing you about!" However, you could still achieve your business objective by bringing your company into your examples and evidence. So your key message might be: "Pupils learn more quickly without calculators", followed by a piece of evidence from a survey you've just conducted about maths teaching. Then you can bring in an example of how your textbooks discourage the use of calculators. (There's more on examples and evidence below.)

Finally, suppose you're representing an academic institution whose ability to attract the best lecturers and researchers has suffered massively in the last few years, but under new leadership is fighting back. In this case, you can be sure that the journalist will be at least as interested in why your organization did so badly in the recent past as in its brighter future. So one of your key messages will need to be a defensive message about the past, supported by one or two positive messages about latest developments. A defensive message might, for example, be: "We were complacent, but we've learned our lesson".

Of course, in this last example you will only want to prepare a defensive message if you're pretty sure that the journalist will focus at least some of the interview on your poor business performance in the past. There is no point in communicating a defensive message if the journalist wants to focus the interview entirely on something positive for your organization.

And therein lies the difference between a key message and a mere answer to a particular question. A key message is something you will proactively seek to communicate *regardless of whether you are asked about it directly*. If you're only planning to communicate something *if asked about it*, then it's not a key message. It's an answer to a question.

Boil your message down to 10 words or fewer

When you are confident that you have a strong message that matters to the journalist's audience, it is vital to boil it down to a few well-chosen words. I always encourage my trainees to limit the number of words that should go into a top-line message to 10, because a short message of 10 words or fewer is so much easier for the audience to remember and act on than a lengthy or complicated one.

In fact, 10 words is quite generous. Jeremy Gutsche, innovation expert and founder of TrendHunter.com, advises companies to use just *seven* words or fewer to define their story. His hallmarks for a good message are that they should be simple, direct and most importantly "supercharged" – ie as impactful as possible. If a message has these hallmarks, says Gutsche, it makes the audience say "I have to tell people about this" and it becomes viral.

In contrast, if you have a wishy-washy message that takes you 200 words and a minute and a half to articulate, the journalist will simply have to summarize your message for you, even live in a broadcast interview. Good journalists do that instinctively, to get to the core of the story. (In a chapter on "Constructing Stories" in her book *Good Writing for Journalists* (2007), Angela Phillips writes: "You should be able to summarize your story in one line".) And in the process, the journalist might make your message more glib or negative than you'd intended. The way to stop that happening, to retain control over it, is to keep it to 10 words or fewer, and then the journalist won't need to summarize it further.

Think of your message like you might the headline in a newspaper. A headline is never very long, but it is unmissable. It stands out. It catches the attention and invites the reader into the article as a whole. That's exactly what your key message should do. You should aim to make it *unmissable*.

Boiling down a message to 10 words or fewer is not always as easy as it sounds. For some people it comes naturally, but for others it can take plenty of time and effort. But it is time well spent. In her training courses one of my media training colleagues, former BBC and LBC presenter Gill Pyrah, invites her trainees to consider the thousands or hundreds of thousands that a company might spend on developing the perfect straplines and slogans for advertising their products. She then points out that they spend all that money only because they know how vitally important those few words are in persuading the audience to act in a certain way.

Likewise, you or your spokesperson should never go into your interview without being sure about your top-line messages. It is the

Great messages

'For the many not the few'

In the mid-1990s, Britain's Labour Party, led by Tony Blair, started communicating this message, which it still uses to this day. It has all the qualities of a good message. It is short, easy to understand, easy to repeat and even, depending on your point of view, inspirational. Regardless of whether you support the Labour Party's policies and ideology, this message is powerful, resonant and difficult for Labour's opponents to argue against.

'There were three of us in this marriage'

Some messages are so powerful that they only need to be said in one interview to go down in history. In 1995, Diana, Princess of Wales, conducted one of the most famous interviews of all time with the BBC's Martin Bashir. Even now, more than 20 years later, it is utterly compelling to watch, no more so than when Diana said about her relationship with Prince Charles: "There were three of us in this marriage, so it was quite crowded". This obviously rehearsed line was like dynamite, and it rocked the British monarchy.

'2012 is going to be the Twitter election'

Dick Costolo, CEO of Twitter, used this line to great effect in interviews in 2012, referring to the US presidential election later that year. By doing so, he cleverly and successfully put his company and its service at the centre of this huge rolling news story.

The best messages look incredibly simple. But a lot of time and effort goes into creating them.

one and only part of your interview that you might want to know off by heart – or close to it. You don't want to lose impact by struggling to find the words, live in the interview. Your top-line message is too important for that.

Ironically, people who are world experts in their field can find it a particular struggle to boil down a message to something short and snappy. Imagine you know everything there is to know about widget design. Boiling down your immense knowledge to two or three key messages about widgets, each of 10 words or fewer, might be a big challenge. In contrast, someone who knows only a little about widget design might find the task more straightforward, because they'll just tell the journalist the few things they know.

Of course, I'm not suggesting that people with vast knowledge shouldn't do interviews on their subject, or hand the task over to people with only a superficial understanding. But they might have to work harder than people with lesser knowledge to construct a good message. Being a world expert doesn't necessarily mean that you'll be a good media interviewee. Far from it.

Give me the proof

So you've developed two or three strong messages of 10 words or fewer, and you've made sure that they matter to the audience. Is that enough for the journalist? Not at all. Because as soon as the journalist hears a message that answers their "So what?" test, they will then say "Give me the proof", or words to that effect.

This is where so many media interviewees and their PR advisers can fall down. They think it's enough to give the journalist an impressive-sounding top-line message, forgetting that the journalist won't necessarily believe or respect that message. The journalist requires proof.

There are three ways that you can offer proof to support your message:

- Explanations;
- Examples (in the form of mind-pictures and short stories);
- Evidence (in the form of numbers and short facts).

Of these, examples are the most important. Evidence is the second most important. And explanations are, usually, the least important.

Explanations

Some messages, and only some, benefit from a brief explanation, rather like some headlines benefit from sub-headings, and the titles of some books, including this one, benefit from a sub-title. For example, not so long ago I interviewed a leading executive in the global campaign to eradicate the horrible practice of female genital mutila-tion. Her key message was: "To end this practice, we need to educate people." And she then supported this with a brief explanatory line: "And that means educating *everyone* in a community, including com-munity elders and other leaders."

That explanation worked and was helpful. But I've also interviewed many executives, particularly in business-to-business companies, who rely far too heavily on explanations at the expense of the more power-ful examples and evidence. For instance, an executive at a consultancy firm specializing in the retail industry might have a good top-line mes-sage for an interview with *Retail Week* magazine of: "Retailers must target their promotions much more precisely". What the journalist needs then is a strong example of how a retailer has done that very thing. But an over-reliance on explanations might lead the executive to meander around the subject, saying: "Retailers must know their customers' wants and needs, and develop an intimate knowledge of them and their behaviours. They can do this by segmenting the audi-ence and identifying patterns of behaviour that lend themselves to certain interventions on behalf of the retailer. These interventions, as a result, can be precisely targeted and then closely monitored . . ." etc.

You can almost see the journalist's eyes glazing over! What the journalist needs is for the interviewee to cut out all this meandering, explanatory guff and get straight into a real example and some com-pelling evidence.

Ronald Reagan once said: "If you're explaining, you're losing". So if you or your spokesperson are going to use explanations, keep them short. And remember that the best messages do not require any explanation because they are *self*-explanatory. The British Labour Party's "For the many not the few" is so good and so immediately understandable that it doesn't require an explanatory line. The same goes for: "There were three in this marriage".

Examples

Examples are often the difference between a good interview and a poor one. They have the power to lift an interview, to elevate it, like a cake being lifted in the oven. All interviews should contain at least one good example and the best interviews contain several. And the most effective examples are so full of human life and colour that they become *mind pictures* that the interviewee paints, which the members of the audience see in their mind's eye. Sometimes, they are short stories, which may be over in a matter of seconds, but have the power to illustrate your message. Radio and TV are the perfect media for storytelling, and get viewers and listeners perking up. A brief story or anecdote, well told, can make a big difference to an interview's payoff.

In his book *Lessons from the Top* (2012) the BBC's Gavin Esler talks about how important it is for leaders to be able to tell such stories: "If they cannot tell stories, then they cannot communicate with their followers. The most effective leaders understand that these stories transcend matters of policy. Storytelling is how their leadership is often defined." Esler then explains how leaders who cannot tell such compelling stories don't last very long.

Here's a great example of someone articulating a mind picture in the form of a short story really well. I've been lucky enough to travel to the Falkland Islands on two occasions to conduct media training for those leading islanders (politicians and other dignitaries) who conduct media interviews about the islanders' right to British sovereignty. One of the most memorable interviews I conducted was with a representative of the Falkland Islands Government on the subject of tourism. His key message was: "The Falklands are a great holiday destination for British people". It was succinct, eye-catching and memorable, and even counter-intuitive and intriguing, given that Britain is about as far away from the Falklands as it's possible to get.

He then went straight into an example and mind picture. He said: "When my wife and I finish work in Port Stanley on a Friday night in summer, and we're pretty tired after a hard week, we get into our Land Rover and drive just a few minutes out of town to the most beautiful, deserted beach you'll ever see. We park the vehicle at the top of the beach, and for as far as we can see there's not another human being or any sign of human development. All we see on the lovely sandy beach, for hundreds of yards in either direction, are hundreds of penguins going about their business. Behind us the sun is just slipping below the hills – a huge red disc. And as we look out to sea, on the horizon, we see dolphins dipping in and out of the waves. We sit back, unwind and take in this scene of splendour and wilderness. That's the escapism you get when you visit the Falklands."

Not only is that a completely accurate picture of what the Falkland Islands are like, but that picture he created will always be with me, partly because it is so powerful and partly because it is so enticing. Even better, the picture was directly relevant to his key message about the Falklands being a great tourist destination. As a journalist, and as a listener, I had to make no great mental leap to work out how the message and example connected to each other. The connection was obvious, as it always should be.

That was a lovely, inspiring example and mind picture. But your mind pictures don't have to be lovely. In fact they can be really disturbing, if it suits your message. Imagine you're doing an interview about the importance of campaigning against forced marriages. The mind picture or story you create might be of a young woman who is taken against her will to a country she's never been to before, where she is enslaved and forced into marrying a man she has never met. She cries herself to sleep every night. That's a horrible mind picture, but may well serve your message and inspire people to join your campaign.

The strongest mind pictures are personal to you, so that you are describing things that you have seen or experienced yourself. For example:

- In an interview about forced marriage, you could describe your experience of meeting a victim of it.

- In an interview about a new service your company offers, you could describe how that service is being used by one of your best customers.

- If you're doing an interview about tree conservation, you could describe how it feels to see a mighty 200-year-old oak tree felled.

If you can describe things that you have personally witnessed, you'll be able to infuse your example with those little extra details, those bits of colour, which really bring it to life, develop a story and make it unforgettable.

I recently interviewed a spokesperson for an embassy in Dubai about the need for visiting tourists to get a licence to drink alcohol – which was news to me. The example she gave was of a couple of visiting businessmen who were stopped by the police and asked for their licence, which the businessmen, of course, had failed to get. They ended up in prison for three days. She described this story with such vivid colour and empathy that it will always remain with me. And as a result I shall never forget her key message about the importance of getting a licence if you want to drink alcohol in Dubai. Once again, the link between the message and the example was obvious.

Of course, it would be wholly unethical for you or your spokesperson to claim to have witnessed something that you haven't, just for the sake of a strong example. In those cases, you must rely on examples that you've heard from other people, or case studies that are in the public domain. With enough preparation, you can still make these examples work for you. But remember, drill down into enough detail that your audience is seeing something in their mind's eye. Only then does an example become a mind picture.

I work with many business-to-business companies that are very cautious about talking about the work they've done for customers, because much of it is confidential. However, they can still talk about that work in a more general sense. Say, for instance, that you're the spokesperson for an IT company, and one of your clients is HSBC bank. You might not be able to talk about HSBC specifically, but you could refer to "an international financial services company". Or if you're doing work for Wal-Mart you might refer to "a global retailer". Of course, it would be better if you could talk about the customer by name, but unless both sides agree that the information can be put in the public domain (something that many companies are sensitive about) you have no choice but to talk only in general terms.

If you've only just launched a new product, service or initiative, which has yet to be used by customers, you can still develop a hypothetical mind picture. Say you're doing an interview on behalf of a company that's just won a contract to develop a high-speed rail link between two major cities in Brazil. You can't give a real mind picture about what it's like to travel on the train, because the line hasn't yet been built. And you can't give an example of how business in Brazil is benefiting from the rail link, because no benefit will be felt for years to come. But you *can* paint a picture of what it *will* be like to travel on the train, the comforts you *will* enjoy and the time you *will* save. And you can ask the audience to imagine themselves running a company, such as a recruitment agency, that does business in both cities and needs to send its staff back and forth between the two all the time.

The final way you can paint a mind picture is through an analogy or metaphor. This is particularly useful for complex subjects. Perhaps you are a spokesperson for a company that makes back-end IT systems, specializes in credit control systems or is involved in heavy industry – subjects that might not lend themselves to pictures. Over the years, I've interviewed spokespeople who have used an array of colourful analogies in their interviews to describe their work in these areas. They don't have to be terribly complicated. For example, a spokesperson for an oil company compared the mechanisms used to monitor remote oil rigs with the controls that children use when playing the latest computer games. Analogies like that make strong mind pictures, bring the subject to life and work well to back up your key message.

Speaking to the BBC *Newsnight* programme in 2013 about airport expansion in the south-east of England, London Mayor Boris Johnson used an aeronautical analogy to express his frustration at the slow pace of the Airports Commission's decision-making progress: "We are currently held in a holding pattern over London", he told Jeremy Paxman, the BBC interviewer. Being held in a holding pattern while waiting for your plane to be given permission to land is a frustration well known to people who fly regularly to London, so it was a particularly well chosen analogy given the subject matter of the interview.

Hillary Clinton also used an analogy to good effect when talking about how Pakistan should deal with terrorists. She said at a press conference in October 2011: "You can't keep snakes in your backyard and expect them to only bite your neighbours. Eventually those snakes are going to turn on whoever has them in the backyard."

Don't be tempted into giving long lists of examples. Examples need depth rather than breadth. So if you give a list, just include three or four items, and then drill down into detail on one of them, allowing yourself to develop a full mind picture. So you might tell the journalist: "A range of blue-chip companies have already started using our personalization technology, including Vodafone, Apple and Microsoft. Vodafone, for example, is using the technology to offer its subscribers vouchers . . ."

The art of storytelling

In his book *Genre: A guide to writing for stage and screen*, film director and communications coach Andrew Tidmarsh shows how the best stories have three key elements: order, chaos and re-order. It's a structure, writes Andrew, that people in western cultures have been using to tell stories for 2,000 years. It's one that grabs and holds our attention and interest.

These stories don't have to be very long, and can easily be used to illustrate a key message in an interview. For example, one of Andrew's stories is of a friend of his, let's call him Bob, who volunteers to work as a waiter on the London Eye each Valentine's Day, serving loving couples with champagne and other treats. One year, a young couple boarded the pod where Bob was working. Five minutes into their journey, with Bob about to serve two glasses of champagne, the young man got down on bended knee, produced a ring and asked the young woman to marry him. But the young woman looked horrified, shook her head and said that she didn't see him as husband material. So there was Bob holding two glasses of champagne in front of an embarrassed young woman and a jilted young man – and still 35 minutes to go before they could all get out of the pod. By the time they did so the couple's relationship was over.

We can see the three key elements of the story very clearly:

1 Order: a happy couple enter a London Eye pod.

2 Chaos: the man's proposal goes horribly wrong.

3 Re-order: they are no longer a couple.

(And the message? If you're going to propose, select your location carefully!)

One of the reasons that spokespeople often struggle with examples is that there are so many to choose from, and they fear that if they give too much information about one example the audience might get the impression that they have no others. Actually, audiences don't tend to see it that way. They recognize that one detailed picture tells a bigger story, just like one detailed picture in a newspaper of a wounded soldier tells the readers the big story of the battle that's just been fought. Nobody gets the impression that only one soldier has been injured in the battle.

Evidence

When you think of evidence, think of what makes a big, impressive number, such as an amount of money or a percentage. These bits of evidence are short and sharp, and contrast nicely with your more discursive examples.

So, talking about tourism in the Falklands, a spokesperson might say that:

- **35,000** people visited the Falklands as tourists last year.
- That's an increase of **22 per cent** on the previous 12 months.
- Tourism is now responsible for **33 per cent** of the economy of the Falklands.

Or, doing an interview about consumer attitudes to mobile technology, you might say:

- According to our last survey, **67 per cent** of people feel that society benefits from mobile technology.
- Globally, **one in every four** people owns a smartphone.
- Smartphones now have **45 per cent** more functionality than they did three years ago.

(These figures are for illustration purposes only.)

You want to go easy with numbers, because if you rattle off too many, too quickly, it'll make the audience feel like they're drinking from a power hose. But a few well-chosen and impressive bits of evidence in the form of numbers or short facts will complement your examples perfectly.

Take time, though, to consider how best to frame your evidence. In their best-selling book *Nudge* (2008), two experts in behavioural economics, Richard Thaler and Cass Sunstein, show how the words you use to describe a statistic can have a big impact on the action that the listener takes. For example, they show that heart patients are more likely to agree to a particular operation if their doctor says: "Of 100 patients who have had this operation, 90 are alive after five years" than if the doctor says "Of 100 patients who have had this operation, 10 are dead after five years." The latter statement tends to put more patients off having the operation, even though its content is identical to the former.

It's also sometimes said that people never properly comprehend a number that's bigger than their own mortgage. So be careful to put your millions, billions and trillions in some sort of context that people will understand. For example, if you're discussing the amount the British government spends on international aid each year (about £10 billion), you will make it more meaningful by adding "That's just over 1 per cent of the government's total expenditure", or "It's about £100 for every person living in the country".

Top-line messages, examples and evidence working together

Examples and evidence work perfectly together to answer the journalist's "Give me the proof" test. Your top-line message answers the "So what?" test. That means that you score a win for the journalist. Now all that remains is to make absolutely certain that your messages also enable you to achieve your business objective.

That's how you develop your content for a media interview. And as I always say to my trainees 90 per cent of your preparation for an interview should be about developing your messages, working up your examples and finding those compelling bits of evidence. That leaves about 10 per cent of your preparation for working out answers to the really tricky questions that the journalist might ask you that aren't directly related to your key messages. That 90 per cent/10 per cent balance is healthy.

Journalists will thank you for preparing your key messages in that way, because all journalists want a story. In fact, there are few things worse for a journalist than interviewing someone who hasn't come to the interview with colourful messages, tailored to the journalist's needs. Veteran journalist Michael Johnson, formerly Moscow correspondent of the Associated Press, says: "It's always obvious to me when I'm faced with an interviewee who has been poorly prepared for the encounter. If I cannot extract something new, different and interesting from the interview it is a waste of everyone's time. I simply will not go to press with warmed-over company bumpf. The solution is good preparation in sync with the publication's style and interests. Anything less is an insult to the journalist's intelligence." Fine words and good advice.

Examples and evidence work particularly well together to allow you to communicate with everyone in the audience, regardless of how they like information to be presented to them. Back in 1981, Roger Sperry was awarded the Nobel Prize for his work on right-brain–left-brain theory. His theory was that the right side of the brain is best at creative tasks, like reading emotions and dealing with images and colour, while the left side is better with logic, language and analytical thinking, and that people tend to have a bias one way or the other.

More recent research by, for example, Dr Jeff Anderson, director of the fMRI Neurosurgical Mapping Service at the University of Utah, has cast doubt on Sperry's theories, contending that both halves of the brain usually work together to perform tasks. However, even this latest research shows that a person's activity can be more pronounced on one side or other. This reflects my own experience of conducting training throughout the world. Some people have a preference for evidence (ie short, sharp facts and statistics) over examples (ie mind pictures and short stories), though nearly everyone can relate to them both. So the best thing is to include a mixture of the two. Paint a picture, but also give concrete scientific evidence.

Constructing a "message sandwich"

Having decided upon your examples and evidence, you or your spokesperson are now in a position to construct the perfect answer to a journalist's question. It's what I call the message sandwich, and it is a powerful way to communicate, not just in media interviews but in all types of communication.

The message sandwich

As Figure 3.1 shows, there are three stages to the message sandwich. First, get that message out in 10 words or fewer, followed if necessary by a brief explanation. Don't wait to be asked by the journalist for an example and/or a piece of evidence. Just go straight into them. Finally, summarize the key message again. All in one answer. It's as simple as that.

In a short broadcast interview of, say, two to three minutes, that message sandwich might take you or your spokesperson just 30 seconds to articulate. In a 20-minute print interview, it might take you a couple of minutes. So you expand or contract the message sandwich according to the length of the interview, and you do so by expanding or contracting your example or introducing two or three examples. However, the top-line message itself must always be 10 words or fewer regardless of the length of the message sandwich.

Structuring your messages as sandwiches is not only a great way of communicating in live interviews, but also in recorded interviews, where you usually have far less control over what is eventually broadcast (see Chapter 4). However, you can still encourage the journalist and editor to broadcast your message in the final cut, as opposed to using something else you said in answer to a particular question, by structuring it as a message sandwich. Clearly, the way to maximize your chance of success is to find out from the journalist the perfect length of soundbite for that particular feature. If the journalist only wants 20 seconds from you, your message sandwich needs to be no more than 20 seconds long.

FIGURE 3.1   The perfect structure to an answer to a journalist's question is the message sandwich

1. Message

2. Explanation/example/evidence

3. Message

SOURCE copyright Robert Taylor Communications

Here's my own 20-second message sandwich about effective media training, with the message in bold:

"**Media training should be short and sweet.** Most of my sessions are for three delegates, and take just four hours. I do their first set of interviews right at the start, with the lights and the camera pointing straight at them to get the adrenaline pumping. **So it's all about brevity and impact.**"

Soundbites

A short message sandwich can also be a "soundbite", which TV and radio producers often need from you when you do a recorded interview. In fact, sometimes they may need a soundbite of just 10 or 15 seconds (even if the interview takes 15 or 20 minutes to record) so you really have to be disciplined in cutting out unnecessary words and practising what you want to say. And soundbites are used by print journalists too, who appreciate spokespeople who can sum up their message in a few eye-catching words.

Make your soundbite as compelling and vivid as possible and deliver it with as much conviction and impact as you can muster.

Here are some famous soundbites, each of which took just a few seconds to deliver:

"Ask not what your country can do for you but rather what you can do for your country." (John Kennedy)

"One small step for man, one giant leap for mankind." (Neil Armstrong)

"The only thing we have to fear is fear itself." (Franklin D Roosevelt)

"The problem with socialism is that you eventually run out of other people's money." (Margaret Thatcher)

"No one would have remembered the Good Samaritan if he'd only had good intentions. He had cash as well." (Margaret Thatcher)

A short soundbite like any of these can be the message itself, or an explanation or example to back up the message. But remember that a great soundbite can also be entirely disadvantageous for the person who uttered it:

"I am not a crook." (Richard Nixon)

"I'd like my life back." (Tony Hayward – see Chapter 9)

> "Read my lips: no new taxes." (George H W Bush)
>
> "There is no such thing as society." (Margaret Thatcher)
>
> If you're going to create a great soundbite, make sure it works in your favour.

The message sandwich is not just a great way to communicate in media interviews, but in many other forms of communication. You might, for example, use it in meetings, presentations and question-and-answer sessions. And in the social media age, where communicating succinctly and with impact is so important, the message sandwich can be powerful in short online videos.

For many years, I've been showing my trainees a clip of a former British politician demonstrating the message sandwich. That politician is Jeffrey Archer, who might not be everyone's favourite public figure, but he happens to be excellent at communicating a message. Back in 2001, Archer was sent to prison for perjury. After he was released, a year or so later, he went on a leading British political discussion programme to talk about prison reform. The first question put to him by the journalist was about how the prison system might prepare prisoners for life outside. Archer's answer was a perfect message sandwich, in which I've put his key message in bold:

"**The big thing is education**. And I'm sure the Home Secretary is very aware of this. If you go to prison and you work in a hospital, or you work cleaning out the lavatories or you work in the gardens, you get £12 a week on average. If you go to education, you get £8 a week. And because 98 per cent of people in prison smoke, and spend their weekly income on cigarettes, they used to say to me, Jeffrey, I'd rather work in the lavatories for £12 than get a better education. Seventy-two per cent of people in prisons at the moment cannot read and write. Wouldn't it be wise to have equal pay for those who want to read and write and those who want to work in the lavatories? [At this point the interviewer interjects to ask him to confirm if this is the quickest, easiest reform.] As a former politician, I'd be bound to say to the Home Secretary that one of the biggest problems he has is money. He has an expenditure which he has to keep to, but surely just putting everyone up to £12 . . . Now on top of that, why not give some sort of incentive especially to the young hooligans who get in and don't know how to read and write. Why not say to them: 'If you go and get an O Level or if you learn to read and write we might have you out a month earlier'. But certainly **education is the vital thing at the moment**."

This answer has all the elements of a strong message sandwich:

1 **The top-line message** – "The big thing is education". It's succinct, and easily understandable, so there is no need for an explanatory line. Instead, Archer goes straight into his example and evidence.

2 **The example** of what it's like to be in prison and the choice prisoners face of doing menial tasks for more money or education classes for less. Archer also brings himself into it, by talking about what prisoners said to him, so we get a mind picture of Archer in prison. In the second half of his answer we get a further mind picture of youngsters in prison considering the possibility of being released early if they get an educational qualification. (Incidentally, Archer's use of the term "O Level" is very dated, since that qualification has been almost entirely phased out, but nobody in the audience is going to worry too much about that.)

3 **The evidence**. Without overdoing it, Archer brings in four numbers all of which help him make his point: £12, £8, 98 per cent and 72 per cent.

4 **The top-line message again** – "Education is the vital thing at the moment".

By delivering his message in the form of a sandwich, Archer simply makes it unmissable. It would be impossible to hear that interview and not get his key point. He also makes the message sandwich look easy, and of course as a former politician he has plenty of experience. But it's more than possible for even a relatively inexperienced inter-viewee, with practice, to deliver their message as a sandwich.

Making your message unmissable, as Archer did, is fundamen-tally important to a successful interview. Remember, your audience is going to take away a message from your interview anyway, but it might be something you didn't intend (such as: "I'd never trust that guy in a million years" or "goodness, that was boring"). But if you make your message unmissable by structuring it as a message sandwich you'll give yourself the very best chance of ensuring that your audience remembers and acts on your message, allowing you to achieve your business objective.

Of course, it's not always possible to construct an answer in the form of a message sandwich. And the journalist may ask questions that don't naturally lend themselves to a sandwich delivery. But every interviewee should aim to get their message out in the form of a message sandwich at some point in the interview, and preferably as near to the start of the interview as possible. An interviewee who does that is on their way to being a top media performer whose messages will resonate with the audience.

Get to the point . . .

. . . For the sake of the journalist

The reason that journalists appreciate a message sandwich is that they love to interview people who get to the point and then illustrate it. It's how journalists themselves think: headline (or key message first), followed by supporting examples and evidence. So instinctive is a journalist's desire for the headline, or key point, first that they can find it intensely irritating to interview people who like to set out the context before finally landing the key point.

In other words, journalists tell stories in a rather different way than we traditionally tell bedtime stories to our children. When we tell stories such as Cinderella to our children, the punchline, if you will, comes at the end: Cinderella marries Prince Charming.

However, imagine the story of Cinderella being reported in a newspaper. The headline might be something like: "Prince marries penniless servant girl", with the end of the story coming first.

So journalists like interviewees to structure their answers like this, with the headline first:

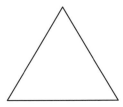

Not like this, with the headline last:

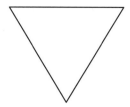

People with a legal or academic bent sometimes find this way of communicating rather alien. They are used to setting out all the facts and putting things in context before then reaching a considered conclusion. But journalists want that considered conclusion first, then the context.

Another reason that journalists, particularly print journalists, like you to get to your key point or headline first is because when they write up your interview into a news story the key questions – Who? What? When? Why? Where? How? – all need to be answered in the first couple of paragraphs.

It should make perfect sense to readers who don't get beyond those two paragraphs, while the newspaper's editors, if they need to make room for other stories, can cut it from the bottom up without losing the meaning.

. . . And for the sake of the audience

Audiences, too, want you to get to the point as quickly as possible, because our attention spans are shorter than they used to be. We make up our minds about something very quickly and simply don't have the patience to sit through lots of context and explanation:

- Research by the US National Institute of Mental Health (2001) concluded that: "Extensive exposure to television and video games may promote development of brain systems that scan and shift attention at the expense of those that focus attention."

- According to internet research company Kissmetrics, 40 per cent of people abandon a website that takes more than three seconds to load.

- In the last 70 years, the average shot length in feature films has gone down from about 10 seconds to under five seconds in order to keep the modern audience engaged and interested. (If you doubt this, watch five minutes of one of the early James Bond films from the '60s, and compare it with the latest ones. The difference is very obvious.)

And if you don't get to the point? Then, just like the journalist, your viewers and listeners will summarize your message for you in their own minds, and might do so in a way that is rather different, and possibly more negative, than you'd intended.

Tell your audience something they didn't know before

American presentation coach, Nancy Duarte, talks about the importance of placing a S.T.A.R. moment (**S**omething **T**hey'll **A**lways **R**emember) in presentations. In her book *Resonate* (2010), she writes: "The S.T.A.R. moment should be a significant, sincere and enlightening moment during the presentation that helps magnify your big idea."

As in presentations, so in media interviews. It should be the ambition of every media interviewee to tell the audience something they didn't know before. Ideally, it should be something jaw-dropping, something that makes the audience go: "Really?" Eliciting the Really? reaction has a number of benefits:

- It makes a broadcast audience more likely to pay attention to the rest of your interview.
- It makes them more likely to report what you said to friends, family and colleagues.
- It makes the journalist more likely to ask you more questions about that subject than negative questions about something else.
- It makes the journalist more likely to want to interview you again.
- It makes it easier to achieve your business objective.

Your Really? material can come in any of the key elements of your message sandwich: the top-line message, the example or the evidence.

Many of my media trainees are competing against spokespeople from other companies to get coverage in the press. The journalist might interview several, but only one or two will be quoted in the final article. Which ones will make the cut? Those that say something unusual, surprising or different. If you merely tell the journalist what everyone else has already said, you make it far too easy for the journalist to leave you out.

For example, if I did an interview about how to deal with awkward delegates during media training sessions, I might try to elicit a Really? reaction by describing how one trainee, after I'd conducted an aggressive crisis media interview with him, shouted at me "You jerk!" (in semi-jest, I like to think, although he did look ready to chin me). Or I might talk about the CEO whose first words to me were that she saw no point in dealing with the media, or doing media interviews, as journalists never reported anything positive about her organization.

Your final message can be a call to action

Many interviews that spokespeople conduct are promotional. That is to say the reason for doing the interview is to promote the organization's products, services or expertise. In these cases, it can often be a good idea for the final message to be a call to action (which is sometimes, but not always, identical to your business objective), such as:

- To find out more, sign up for our newsletter.
- To apply for this scholarship, visit our website.
- Come along to our open day next weekend.

In each of these cases, you can still use examples and evidence. You might, for example, describe what people will see when they sign up for your newsletter, visit your website or come to your open day. Remember, your message isn't complete unless it is backed up with such proof points. A 10-words-or-fewer top-line message needs examples and/or evidence to give it the best chance of being remembered and acted upon.

Ending on a call to action has another benefit: it fits the natural flow of questions from a journalist, which can often end with a "so what happens next?" or "where do people go to find out more?" question. Your call to action is the perfect response.

Remembering your messages

You have two or three beautifully prepared message sandwiches ready to communicate. You've ensured that for each one the top-line message matters to the audience and is 10 words or fewer. You've got enough human colour in your examples that they will create a full mind picture for each member of the audience. And you have a couple of compelling bits of evidence in the form of numbers and statistics.

But then it all goes wrong. I've lost count of the number of times during my training sessions that very senior executives and politicians have simply forgotten their messages in the heat of the interview. Sure, they'll still be able to answer questions, but often their answers are completely unrelated to their key messages. The result is that they fail to hit their stated business objective for the interview. They are helping the journalist but forgetting to help themselves.

So how do you ensure that you remember your messages once the interview starts?

For many interviews it is perfectly permissible for you to have your messages in note form in front of you so you can consult them during the interview. Such interviews include:

- Phone interviews;
- Face-to-face print interviews;
- Radio interviews (unless you're being recorded by web camera).

But you have to make sure that your notes are helpful. There is no point going into an interview with reams and reams of notes, full of dense text. That would be like going swimming with all your clothes on. I once saw the interview notes prepared for a government minister by members of his staff. They must have run to about 5,000 words, dense with facts and figures. They were, in that form, completely unusable.

In contrast, Figure 3.2 illustrates what I consider to be the perfect set of notes for a media interview.

FIGURE 3.2 Make your interview notes easy to use

3 key messages in full	1. Message in full	2. Message in full	3. Message in full
Message	Prompt	Prompt	Prompt
Example	Prompt	Prompt	Prompt
Evidence	Prompt	Prompt	Prompt
Message	Prompt	Prompt	Prompt

This set of notes should all be on one sheet of paper, so that you're not flicking through the pages as the interview progresses, when your attention should be on the journalist.

Have your key messages written out in full across the top of the page. That's important, because in the minutes before you start the interview, you want to be sure that you've got the wording close to word-perfect in your head. Underneath each of those top-line messages you have a series of prompt phrases that you can glance at, which will guide you through your message sandwich.

So, for example, Jeffrey Archer's notes for his key message about education might follow the structure shown in Table 3.1.

TABLE 3.1 Key messages about education

Top-line message	Education is the vital thing
Message prompt	Education
Example prompt	Belmarsh (the name of the prison he was taken to at the start of his sentence)
Evidence prompt	72% can't read (representing the proportion of UK prisoners who can't read and write)
Message prompt	Education

Go through the same process for your other messages, and then you are left with a series of prompt words on a single piece of paper that guide you through the interview and give you the very best chance of staying on track.

Of course, there are some types of interview where it would be unwise to refer to notes. These include:

- Any TV interview, live or recorded.
- Video podcasts.
- Any radio interview where you're being recorded on webcam.

In these instances, the audience will trust you less if they see you consulting your notes. So by all means have them close by so that you can refer to them for one last time in the moments before you go on air. But put them away during the interview itself.

That means that for TV or video interviews you have to commit your key messages to memory, which is one of the things that makes those interviews more stressful than any other. Some people are lucky enough to have photographic memories, but most of us need to work hard to learn our prompt phrases so that they are in the front of our minds during our interview.

Is there a danger that learning your top-line messages off by heart, or close to it, might make you sound too scripted and artificial? No, because although top-line messages are absolutely vital parts of the interview, they take only a short amount of time to communicate. Mind pictures take far longer, and they should never be scripted for that very reason. In fact, it is only when those mind pictures *do* appear scripted that the interviewee begins to lose authenticity.

Is there another way?

About one in 20 of the people I train just can't stick to the discipline of having two or three key messages. Their minds don't work that way and there's no point in forcing them. What they require is a menu of messages, or a mind map of messages, that they can pick and choose from depending on how the interview progresses and the questions the journalist asks.

There are, however, disadvantages to that approach. It means that, to be properly ready for their interview, the interviewee needs to do far more preparation. After all, it will take far longer to prepare, say, 10 messages with good examples and evidence than it will take to prepare two or three. It also means that they rule themselves out of certain types of interviews. For instance, a company's PR department will often task a spokesperson with communicating one or two particular messages during an interview about the company's financial results. Unless a spokesperson has the discipline to stick to those messages, they cannot be put in front of a journalist – just like an actor can't go on stage unless they can be trusted to deliver their lines.

However, not all is lost for those one in 20 people who prefer to pick and choose messages from a menu structure; there are plenty of interviews where they can still be effective advocates for their organization. One of my recent trainees, a vice president of finance for a global company, did a superb TV interview with me about how women should aim to reach the top of big companies. She used herself as a mind picture and spoke about her own experiences and the lessons she learned on the way to the senior leadership team of her company.

Less is more

It is far better to communicate one message well than to shoehorn in two or three and do none of them justice. This is especially true of a short broadcast interview of, say, 90 seconds, when it would be madness to try to communicate three, or possibly even two, key messages. Don't try to cram too much into an interview or your audience will simply tune out.

The media is an environment for simplicity, not complexity. Andrew Marr, former BBC political editor, wrote about this in his book *My Trade: A short history of British journalism* (2004): "Journalists learn to take less extraordinary things and fashion them into words that will make them seem like news instead . . . They reshape life, cutting away details, simplifying events, 'improving' ordinary speech, sometimes inventing quotes, to create a narrative which will work."

And Alfred Harmsworth, founder of the UK's *Daily Mail* newspaper, said, even more succinctly, that a journalist is there to "Explain, simplify, clarify."

Knowing that the journalist is striving for simplicity, it makes sense for you to help them.

Summary

1 Decide your business objective and make it an action that you want the audience to take.

2 Develop no more than three key messages that help you achieve your business objective.

3 Make sure your messages matter to the journalist's readers, viewers or listeners.

4 Boil them down to 10 words or fewer.

5 Provide proof points in the form of examples and evidence.

6 Make sure that your examples have enough detail to become mind pictures.

7 Consider whether analogies might help you get your point across.

8 Practise delivering your messages, examples and evidence as message sandwiches.

9 Put your notes for your interview all on one page.

10 Tell your audience something that makes them think "Really?"

Exercises

1 Think of an interview that you or a spokesperson from your organization might be invited to do. What would make a good action-orientated business objective?

2 What two or three key messages might you decide to communicate in that interview? Do they pass the journalist's "So what?" test?

3 What sort of examples and evidence might you use to support your key messages?

4 How could you develop each message into a "message sandwich"?

5 Try to boil down your messages to a series of prompt words on a single sheet of paper.

Keeping your cool

04

In this chapter we discuss mechanisms for maintaining an even temper during a media interview. This means maintaining a healthy degree of adrenaline, because too much or too little can land you or your spokesperson in all sorts of trouble. It means keeping calm whatever the provocation, and it means showing passion and assertiveness, but not anger.

Too much adrenaline – nervousness

You might think that nervousness is something that only beginners have to deal with. But that's not always the case. Even experienced interviewees can face an uncomfortable adrenaline surge, which, in extreme cases, can leave them almost speechless.

In 2010, one of Tony Blair's former aids, the vastly experienced Alastair Campbell, gave a live TV interview to BBC journalist Andrew Marr. During the interview, Marr asked Campbell whether Tony Blair had misled parliament in the run-up to the Iraq war. As this question was being asked, Campbell breathed heavily (and not, it appears healthily – see section on breathing exercises below), and when he started speaking his voice was thinner and more high-pitched than normal. He took a deep breath (again, it appeared to be an unhealthy one) to try to recover his poise. He then ground to a halt.

It makes for uncomfortable viewing (Google: "emotions get the better of Alastair Campbell") and anyone who has experienced hyperventilation, for that's what it looked like, knows how horrible it can feel. You literally run out of breath and are therefore incapable of saying anything. To Campbell's credit he recovered fairly quickly and completed the interview.

But the point is this: if too much adrenaline can affect an experienced spokesperson like Campbell, it can happen to many others too. It's vital, therefore, to keep that adrenaline at acceptable limits – to keep those nerves under control.

My media trainees are usually only too aware of this. At the start of every training session, I always ask people for their objectives, and around 50 per cent of delegates say that one of their main aims is dealing with a lack of confidence. This is entirely understandable. Doing a media interview is, by its very nature, a bit of a risk as well as a fantastic opportunity:

- You are handing a good portion of control over to the journalist, who is usually a complete stranger to you.
- In a print or recorded-broadcast interview, there is always the danger that your words will be taken out of context (though you can minimize the danger by following the guidelines in Chapter 3).
- In a live broadcast interview spokespeople fear that they might stumble over their words, dry up or say something foolish.
- In some cases, a journalist might be deliberately provocative and aggressive.
- Once published or broadcast the interview is probably going to be up on the internet for ever and a day.

In short, doing a media interview can be scary. A broadcast interview is particularly so, and a *live* broadcast interview tops the pile.

So why, then, do I like hearing at the start of a session that my delegates are a little nervous? Simply because they usually end up being really good at doing media interviews – because they take nothing for granted, never come across as arrogant or dismissive and are keen to do it well.

In fact, of the thousands of people I've trained over the last decade, I can only remember one who was so racked with nerves as to be simply untrainable. Everyone else has not only coped with the nervous energy coursing through their bodies, but has improved considerably, using the energy to their advantage.

Mechanisms for boosting your confidence

These guidelines are mainly for the broadcast environment, but can also apply to print interviews.

1 Remember that the journalist usually wants to help you

Even during Alastair Campbell's mini breakdown you can hear Andrew Marr in the background trying to encourage him and support him when he hits his sticky moment.

It's rarely in the journalist's interest for you to be a nervous wreck because interviewees perform much better and help the journalist create a better piece of television or radio if they are relaxed.* In fact, in *The Broadcast Journalism Handbook*, editors Gary Hudson and Sarah Rowlands advise broadcast journalists to "put your interviewee at ease" and "reassure people . . . that they will be treated fairly and your intentions are sincere . . . They need to have confidence that you are professional and know what you are doing."

Former BBC and LBC presenter Gill Pyrah agrees: "If you've got three minutes allocated on national radio or seven-plus minutes on local, there's absolutely no advantage for the interviewer in having the interviewee be a bundle of nerves and grinding to a halt, leaving minutes to fill. Unless the interviewee is a cocky celebrity who's suddenly tongue-tied it's uncomfortable for listeners and viewers too if the poor guest is falling apart, and certainly the presenter doesn't want to risk them turning to another channel. Listener and viewer figures (on which the presenter's next contract depends) will show when an audience is switching off mid-show: the idea is to build an audience as the show goes along, not lose it. So have your first answer ready and be determined to bridge to it, whatever the question. If

---

Although this is a safe rule of thumb, there are rare occasions where this isn't the case, and we'll discuss these more a little later in this chapter.

you tell me something interesting, that isn't blindingly obvious or a blatant advertisement, I'll do what I can to keep you on track and happy."

2 Remind yourself that you are the expert

When a journalist is asking you questions, particularly in a broadcast environment, it's all too easy to lapse back into school-exam mode and think you're being *tested* – that it's all about passing or failing. Try not to look at it like that. In most cases the journalist wants to interview you because of your knowledge of or expertise in the subject being discussed. You know more about the subject than they do and your knowledge and expertise will help the journalist develop a good story.

There are vast numbers of confidence-boosting exercises that you can try. And the best are often the simplest. In her book *Total Confidence* (1994) Philippa Davies advises "keeping a valuable bank of achievements we are proud of" and simply writing these achievements down. The mere act of doing so will give you a tremendous confidence boost, as will studying your list of achievements before the interview starts.

There are many more confidence-raising activities that you can find with a simple internet search. For example:

- The website Uncommon Help (www.uncommonhelp.me/articles/how-to-build-self-confidence/) offers seven top tips for building confidence, ranging from not taking yourself too seriously to self-hypnosis.
- Mind Tools (http://www.mindtools.com/selfconf.html) advises you to go on a confidence-boosting "journey", starting with Preparation, then Setting Out and finally Accelerating Towards Success.
- Oprah Winfrey's website (http://www.oprah.com/spirit/Quick-Confidence-How-to-Boost-Self-Esteem) offers "11 ways to boost your self-esteem in less than an hour".

Clearly it's important, as with everything on the internet, to find what works for you.

3 Practise

How did Gary Player become a great golfer? By hitting tens of thousands of balls in practice. He famously said: "The more I practise the luckier I get".

Likewise, you or your spokesperson can't expect to give a great media interview unless you've had a few dry runs, preferably in a full media-training session. Practice interviews don't just sharpen up your delivery, they also flush out the messages that work well, those that should be binned and those that need tweaking.

Gill Pyrah says: "A lack of preparation can be catastrophic for the interviewee. One interviewee who was invited on LBC at almost no notice to fill a suddenly vacant 20-minute slot was so nervous that after a few minutes she simply stopped trying to speak and slid under the desk. Sweat was dribbling off her forehead and I thought she was going to be sick. Though I was being as helpful as I could, I hadn't had any briefing, other than she'd had a film script picked up by Hollywood. I had to limp on with the interview, which descended into: 'You are nodding so you seem to agree with that'. I felt desperately sorry for the poor woman, who obviously had absolutely nothing prepared. What should have been a great opportunity to advertise her skills was instead a blistering ordeal."

You might also consider using a neuro-linguistic programming (NLP) technique called Perceptual Positions, which involves imagining the interview situation from a range of perspectives, including the journalist's and the audience's. By looking at it from, literally, different angles, Perceptual Positions helps you to examine the situation in a much more balanced way, visualize the outcome you want and therefore keep that adrenaline at a healthy and helpful level.

4 Voice exercises

When you are nervous you can get jittery and tongue-tied, stumbling over words and simply failing to articulate properly, so that the audience is left struggling to hear. It's rather like the sensation you get when trying to speak clearly on an icy winter's day: the tongue and mouth muscles seem to seize up, and the inarticulate result is not only distracting for the audience but can even lead to doubts about your competence.

The trick here is to get everything lubricated and running smoothly, just as actors do before they go on stage. There are literally thousands of voice exercises you can do (just Google "voice exercises for actors"), but here are a few of my favourites from actor and voice coach Isabel Russo:

- *The thumb in the mouth.* Grip the upper part your thumb (from nail to first joint) in a vertical position between your teeth, and then try to read out a paragraph or two of text from anything that happens to be to hand. The mouth and tongue muscles have to work so hard to do this with the thumb as an obstacle that when you take your thumb out of your mouth, you find yourself speaking with wonderful resonance and articulation. (NB This exercise is excellent but it can make you look a bit silly, so do it somewhere private!)

- *Tongue twisters.* Try repeating any favourite tongue twister over and over again, such as "Red lorry yellow lorry", "Peter Piper picked a peck of pickled peppers", "She sells sea shells on the sea shore" or simply "athletic articulation". As you do so, try to enunciate each syllable as clearly as possible.

- *Yawning.* Stretch up to the ceiling and consciously yawn as widely as you possibly can. This releases tension and opens up the throat, enabling you to speak with resonance and freedom.

Russo says: "To be an effective communicator, you need to be in control of your material and aware of the physical and vocal messages you are giving on every level. All emotions trigger physical reactions. Emotional tension reads in the voice and can play havoc. Repeated tensions can set up bad habits and lead to more developed problems, from a dry mouth and breathlessness to back ache.

"I believe that the voice is one of the most intimate things about a person. It reveals so much in just a few seconds. On a subliminal level it reveals who we are, who we are trying to be and who we are trying not to be. The body and the voice are intrinsically linked, and tension and tiredness in the body reads in the voice. When we wake up the body we wake up the mind and when the voice is warmed up and centred we are able to connect with ourselves more powerfully and deliver our message more effectively.

"A good warm up doesn't need to be long. Even just spending five minutes doing a few exercises that work for you, including stretching, deep breathing and humming, can make a big difference."

5 Breathing exercises

Breathing exercises are useful for everyone, but particularly people who tend to get nervous before interviews and presentations. This is incredibly important, because healthy breathing is the root of good, strong, confident inter-personal communication. In contrast, unhealthy breathing can lead to a constrained voice and in some cases, as Alastair Campbell seems to have experienced, hyperventilation.

To tell if you are breathing healthily put your hand on your stomach and feel it going in and out. Your hand should be moving out when you breathe in and in when you breathe out. It sounds easy. It sounds natural. But amazingly enough lots of people do it the wrong way round and as a result their voices don't carry nearly the warmth, confidence and authority they should. What's more, they miss out on the release of endorphins that healthy breathing encourages, which is so helpful for controlling nerves.

Just as with voice exercises, there are lots of breathing exercises on the internet that will help get you primed and full of confidence for your interview. But here are a few of my favourites recommended by Adrienne Thomas, a voice coach for the UK's Royal Academy of Dramatic Art (RADA):

- Drop down through the spine, letting the crown of the head lead the other vertebrae down, one at a time, so that you're bent double. Hanging over from the tailbone, become aware of each new breath dropping into the middle of your body. Then curl up slowly through the spine one vertebra at a time from the sacrum upwards, letting the neck vertebrae come up last, floating the head on top of the spine.

- Breathe out through lightly parted lips. You'll find that the friction of the air passing between them will result in a loose, sloppy FFF sound (although there is no actual voiced vibration). Then just wait for a moment or two, without tensing the belly muscles. Have a hand on your breathing centre, around the belly button. Wait until you yield to the need for a new breath, and then breathe in deeply, feeling your stomach going out. Try this a few times and you should find that the breath begins to drop low into the body. It's the moment of waiting, daring to do nothing, that enables the deep release of the breath.

- Let the breath drop deep into the belly a few times. As you breathe out, sigh on a voiced HUUH and draw vibrations from belly to chest with your hands. Thump the chest and really feel the vibrations there. Continue voicing on "HUUUUH", then "HUH-HUH" and "HUH-HUMMM" onto a hum. You can try on different pitches as well, within the lower to middle parts of your range, to open up vocal variety. Picture your vibrations releasing from your chest into the space beyond you. Then try with some words, such as a few lines from a favourite poem or a story from the newspaper, or something interesting that you really want the interviewer to know.

Adrienne Thomas says: "A low breath is the key to being in control of nerves rather than letting them be in control of us. It's no coincidence that Yoga and Tai Chi focus on releasing the breath low into the body. Not only does a low breath help release unnecessary physical tension, it is also the fuel for the voice and will help us to sound more confident and committed to what we are saying. In addition, paying attention to the breath actually increases focus and awareness, so it has important benefits for our state of mind."

Do a few breathing exercises in the minutes before your interview starts and you'll feel much less stressed and much more confident.

Under the spotlight

Going into a TV or a radio studio for a live interview can be daunting. Doing an interview on location is only slightly less nerve-racking. Here's how some who have experienced broadcast interviews have coped with the pressure.

Duncan Sedgwick, Chief Executive of the UK's Energy Retail Association from 2003 until 2008

As the head of the association representing gas and electricity companies Sedgwick was often asked to do live and recorded national TV and radio interviews to explain and defend the energy bills that consumers paid. Not surprisingly, he was often portrayed as the "baddie" by the broadcasters, and got used to being subjected to hostile and aggressive interviews.

"The key thing is to know your stuff and remember the five Ps: 'Proper Planning Prevents Poor Performance'. Even if I was going to be on air for only a minute, I'd take time to prepare thoroughly and work out pretty much exactly what I was going to say. I'd close my eyes before I went live into the studio, and get myself into the right mindset, visualizing what I was going to say. Then, from the moment I walked into the studio, even before the interview had started, I'd assume that anything I said could be broadcast, so I was essentially in interview mode from that moment on. And I'd stay in interview mode until I left the building. I would leave nothing to chance, and say nothing that I might be embarrassed by if it was picked up by a stray microphone.

"In the studio, whether TV or radio, I'd concentrate, concentrate, concentrate. Broadcast programmes, even when discussing serious topics like energy prices, are essentially about entertainment for the audience, and I was well aware that the presenter would be happy to make a fool of me if it made good TV or radio. One slip, one loose expression, might ruin the whole interview from my point of view. I knew I was playing on their pitch, so I wasn't ever arrogant enough to think I could beat them at their own game, but I always aspired to a score draw.

"I'd always have three points to make, and having answered the journalist's first question I'd go straight into my first point, without hesitation. That gave me some control over a situation that was often very intimidating. I remember the first time I ever went into the BBC Radio 4 *Today Programme* studio [the most high-profile morning radio programme in the UK] and seeing John Humphrys sitting across from me, and suddenly being struck by the enormity of what I was doing: a live interview on a sensitive topic with one of the country's most famous and feared interviewers, and knowing I was going to be heard by millions of people throughout the country.

"But I quickly learned to block out such thoughts and narrow my focus to the presenter or reporter who was asking me the questions. Sometimes this was easier than at other times, and I had to be ready for anything. One radio reporter asked me a question in a live interview, and promptly walked out of the studio – to go to the toilet he casually told me later – so I was delivering my answer to thin air. A famous BBC Radio 5 Live presenter would put his feet up on the desk in front of me during our interview, presumably to unnerve me. And a presenter on GMTV [national TV breakfast show watched by millions] whispered to me just before my interview with her was due to start 'I'm going to get you.' I thought to myself: 'No you bloody aren't'.

"At the same time, it's vital never to lose your rag, even under intense provocation, because it'll just make you look like an idiot. So I always tried to keep my cool. I remember Sky News coming to talk to me once in my own home, and we did the interview in my conservatory overlooking the garden. But that didn't stop the reporter from immediately going on the attack. The very first question I got from him was this: 'What does it feel like to be the most unpopular man in Britain?' That question was designed to throw me off track and rile me, even in my own home, so it was important not to rise to the bait."

Steve Marsh, spokesperson for the Woodland Trust

Steve represents the UK's leading woodland conservation charity, and has carried out interviews on a range of regional and national TV and radio broadcasts. Steve usually has good-news stories to tell, and even when he doesn't, the broadcasters are rarely hostile. But that doesn't necessarily make things easier, because the onus is on Steve to make the story as interesting as possible for the viewers and listeners. Like Duncan Sedgwick, Steve emphasizes the vital importance of preparation:

"The key thing is to be prepared and know what you're going to say. For my first interview on BBC *Breakfast TV*, on the sofa in the studio, I spent the entire two-hour car journey on my way to the studio going over and over what I wanted to say, so that by the time

I got there I had done the interview about 100 times in my head. I didn't want the first time I thought about my answer to a particular question to be live on air!

"Being able to bridge to your key messages [see Chapter 7] is absolutely crucial, because a question might come in a hundred different forms but there's always a way you can bridge to what you want to say. In fact, your message can be the right answer to lots of different questions, and knowing that gives you confidence.

"I'd also advise any interviewee not just to prepare what you think you *need* to know, but what the audience would *expect* you to know. So, for example, I clearly need to know about tree preservation, but the audience would also expect me to know about woodland animals and plants.

"Being confident about your material means that you are much better able to cope with the other big challenge with broadcast interviews: the sheer variety of settings. I've been interviewed in the middle of muddy woods in the wind and rain, on a busy city street with lots of people going past, perched on a stool in a tiny outside-broadcast van, in a sound-booth doing a "down-the-line" interview with national radio, and of course on a sofa in a TV studio. All present their own physical challenges, and it's far easier to adapt to those challenges if you're completely 100 per cent on top of your material.

"For my interview on BBC *Breakfast TV*, on the sofa in the studio, I arrived at 6.45am, and was on air by 7.20am, so there wasn't much time. But the producers were brilliant, and made a point of making me feel welcome and settled. Essentially, I was working with them to create what we all wanted to be a good piece of TV, complete with pictures of various wildlife. So they were keen for me to say things in a particular order so that they could put images on the screen while I was talking. It actually felt like quite a controlled environment, and I treated the interview as a conversation, which made it much easier."

Jamie Bartlett, Director of the Centre for the Analysis of Social Media at DEMOS
National and international broadcasters often interview Bartlett because of his expertise on subjects such as new political movements, internet cultures, and security and privacy online.

"The more broadcast interviews I've done, particularly in a studio setting, the more I've got used to what seems at first to be a foreign environment. For example, you are often brought into the studio with only a minute before your interview starts, and you find that the presenter is gabbling away to the producers behind the glass, but looks as though they're talking to thin air. Then suddenly their tone switches to being the inquisitor when they are back on air, and you are their focus. All these little things can take you by surprise when you're not used to it and knock you off balance.

"The single most important piece of advice I'd give anyone is to prepare your first answer, so you know exactly where you want to take the interview right at the start. And of course that means asking, before the interview starts, what the first question will be [see Chapter 7]. Then just think of it as a conversation, in which you are trying to make simple points clearly and with plenty of expression in your voice.

"When I first started doing live interviews, as opposed to pre-records, I noticed how I'd be too careful with what I was saying, because, with only one shot at it, I was so keen not to make a mistake or say something I'd regret. But that cautious approach doesn't engage the audience nearly so well, so I've now learned to be bolder and more assertive in live interviews, to give myself the very best chance of making it interesting and newsworthy for the listeners and viewers. There's no use in playing it so safe that nobody pays any attention."

Too much adrenaline – anger

We've discussed how journalists don't want interviewees to be nervous wrecks. However, an interviewee who gets *angry* is another matter altogether. Even if they don't typically go looking for anger, or try to provoke it, journalists know that it can make great TV. And the interviewee nearly always ends up the loser.

In 1993, an Australian government minister, Max Ortmann, brought a violent end to an interview with ABC's reporter Jeremy Thompson. Ortmann had agreed to the interview following suggestions that he had acted inappropriately in giving the go-ahead for a new building scheme in Darwin Harbour to a developer who had helped get him elected to parliament three years previously.

Ortmann began to lose his self-control control when Thompson asked him whether he thought there was a conflict of interest and whether a man who had helped him get his seat in parliament "should be a recipient of government largesse". This is how the interview then went:

Thompson:	Do you reject that the public could see your involvement with [name of developer] and the approval given to Bay View Haven as another "jobs for the boys"?
Ortmann:	No. Absolutely ridiculous. Anyone who puts that to air or states that publicly will have to be very careful.
Thompson:	Why's that?
Ortmann:	Because I think you're trying to defame me.
Thompson:	In what way, I'm sorry?
Ortmann:	You're trying to draw conclusions that are incorrect and way off mark. [Ortmann's voice cracks.] And I reject it totally and you can finish the interview now and get out.
Thompson:	I'm not trying to say that there was anything illegal happening whatsoever . . . [Ortmann leans forward picks up the microphone that was on his desk and throws it across the room.] . . . but what I am saying . . . what I am saying . . .
Ortmann:	[Ortmann stands up and walking around the desk towards Thompson.] Out. Come on, had enough, out. [Pulls Thompson's notes from his pad and screws them up.]
Thompson:	Why's that?
Ortmann:	Because I reject what [inaudible]. Now get out.
Thompson:	Isn't this a bit of an overreaction, sir?

Ortmann:	[Standing up and pointing at Thompson's face.] No, I don't like being accused of the corruption you're talking about.
Thompson:	I'm not talking about corruption . . .
Ortmann:	Out.
Thompson:	I'm not alleging . . .
Ortmann:	Come on, off you go.
Thompson:	I'm not alleging any illegality whatsoever . . .
Ortmann:	Off you go. Off you go. Off you go.
Thompson:	What about our receptionist?
Ortmann:	[Yanking out the microphone wires.] I don't care about the receptionist. Out! [Ortmann wraps the microphone wire around Thompson's upper body, towards his neck, then pulls it violently.] You're being ordered out of a minister's office, alright. OUT! Now get out, and I mean get out.
Thompson:	[Untangling the wire from around his body and neck.] Alright, we're going.
Ortmann:	You garbage heap.

This is by far the angriest, most violent and most dramatic interview I've ever seen, and the transcript doesn't do justice to it. To see the full horror, Google "Australian minister Max Ortmann." And yet, although it was a painful, not to say frightening experience for Thompson, he was the winner. It remains, more than 20 years later, a superb bit of TV, and he is still with ABC.

The loser? That would be Ortmann. After the incident, he earned the nickname "Mad Max" and he quickly lost his seat in parliament.

Excessive anger simply alienates people, because it reveals someone who is, in the words of John Neffinger and Mathew Kohut in their book *Compelling People*, ". . . out of control, unable to handle the challenges of their environment in a functional, clearheaded way."

By all means be assertive and strong. By all means refute allegations that you believe to be wrong and unfair, but maintain control over yourself and your emotions. If a journalist interrupts you, don't interrupt back or try to talk over them. Let them ask their question, and then calmly state that you'd like to finish the point you were making first.

US media expert Carole Howard wrote in *Public Relations Quarterly* (Winter 2002): "Some interviewers deliberately frame questions in emotional or accusatory terms, going for 'attitude' or 'edge' in their story. It is just a tactic to get you to say something controversial. Don't let it work."

Carol Rosenbaum, US-based communications adviser, agrees. She wrote in *Tactics* magazine (December 2007): "Don't take hostile questions personally . . . Allowing your ego to be bruised telegraphs weakness and raises questions about your competence under duress. In fact, a hostile question can be an opportunity to show mental agility and grace under fire."

Yet although all this advice makes perfect sense, public figures continue to fall into the anger and frustration trap, often egged on by the journalist. They usually regret it:

- In 2011, experienced British politician and government minister Ken Clarke allowed himself to get into a heated argument with national radio broadcaster Victoria Derbyshire about the nature of rape. When Derbyshire put it to Clarke that "rape is rape" Clarke testily replied "No, it is not . . ." He spent the next few days apologizing and battling to save his job, while Derbyshire received plenty of plaudits for producing a compelling piece of radio.

- Also in 2011 the chief executive of Research in Motion (RIM), Mike Lazaridis, accused the BBC during a recorded interview of asking unfair questions about his company's activities in India. Getting visibly agitated and angry, and shaking his head as questions were put to him, he ended the interview pointing to the camera and saying: "Turn that off". The result? The BBC broadcast the interview anyway and RIM's market share continued to slide.

- In 2013, British politician Godfrey Bloom had his own "Mad Max" moment when he responded to questioning from BBC journalist Michael Crick by hitting him over the head with a conference brochure. He resigned a few days later. (Google "Godfrey Bloom hits Michael Crick"). To be fair to Bloom, he'd had it coming anyway. He'd already been recorded giving a speech in which he jokingly described the women in his audience as "sluts".

In all these cases, the journalist gained through the subsequent publicity, whereas the interviewee lost. And it's also important to remember an interviewee doesn't need to go through a full tantrum to come across as angry. The watching or listening audience will be quick to pick up on the slightest flicker of annoyance or temper, which will then colour the whole interview like a drop of ink in a glass of water.

In nearly all circumstances keep your cool, even when the journalist is riling you. It's simply not worth losing it.

So should you ever lose your cool?

Notwithstanding anything in the section above, there are occasions when it would look very odd and seem entirely unnatural if you didn't lose *a little of* your cool.

Running for US president in 1988, the Democratic candidate Michael Dukakis was asked this question by Bernard Shaw of CNN during a live TV debate: "Governor, if Kitty Dukakis [his wife] were raped and murdered would you favour an irrevocable death penalty for the killer?"

Now, we can of course argue endlessly about the merits and ethics of such a question. But as we discuss elsewhere in this book, journalists *do ask unfair questions from time to time*, and there's not a lot you can do to stop them. But you have complete control over how you respond.

So how should Dukakis have responded to a question that asked him to consider the rape and murder of his own wife? How would *any* husband *naturally* respond? Surely we'd have expected him to be visibly shocked at the suggestion, even as the question were being put to him, and to register his horror at the very idea. Perhaps he would have physically recoiled a little, and said something like: "I think that's a terrible thing for any husband to consider, and frankly I think I'd respond just like any other person would to the death of a loved one. It's probably the worst thing that can happen to you . . ."

Instead of which Dukakis, completely unruffled and composed as the question was asked, said: "No, I don't, and I think you know that I've opposed the death penalty during all of my life; I don't see any evidence that it's a deterrent and I think there are better and more effective ways to deal with violent crime, and we've done so . . ."

This one passionless moment, many commentators thought, set Dukakis on the path to eventual defeat to George Bush in that election.

Controlled passion is what to go for. But it can be a difficult judgement call. During the UK's 2001 general election campaign, a member of the public threw an egg at Labour's deputy prime minister, John Prescott, at point-blank range right in front of the cameras. Prescott responded by launching a punch at the perpetrator's face and then brawling with him on the ground before police intervened (Google "Prescott punches voter"). Yet the episode did little to damage Prescott, politically-speaking, nor the Labour Party, presumably because most voters thought that his reaction was fairly understandable.

The exceptions

Legendary football manager Sir Alex Ferguson routinely lost his temper with reporters, even during after-match interviews with TV. For example, after his team, Manchester United, lost the 2011 European Cup Final to Barcelona he directed a brief but unmistakable "hairdryer blast" at ITV reporter Gabriel Clark, who had the temerity to ask what the team would have to work on to match Barcelona's high standards. Ferguson also refused to speak to the BBC's *Match of the Day* programme for years, and even once had a set-to with inoffensive BBC commentator John Motson.

But Ferguson was in an unusual position. Manchester United's consistent success under his leadership and passionate, global following meant that journalists needed him more than he needed them. The same, of course, goes for managers of other top football clubs, but Ferguson appeared to have a particularly short fuse.

Are there others in this enviable position of being needed by the media more than they need them? Well, Prince Philip might be one, if only because he's now in his tenth decade of life. He was pretty surly towards BBC presenter Fiona Bruce when she interviewed him to mark his 90th birthday, at one stage casting doubt on whether her chosen occupation, journalism, is a profession – which was hardly the subject of the interview. (It was later reported that the prince was expecting to be interviewed by Selina Scott and was irritated that it was Bruce instead.)

But Ferguson and Prince Philip are among the few who can get away with anger and irritability on camera. For executives and spokespeople from nearly all other organizations, who need the media at least as much as the media needs them, the rule when doing interviews is straightforward: try to be nice and keep calm.

Not enough adrenaline – over-confidence

Not surprisingly, and notwithstanding Alastair Campbell's stumble on the Andrew Marr show, over-confidence and being too relaxed tends to be an issue for experienced interviewees rather than for novices. And it can cause a big problem when it leads you into saying things without thinking through the consequences – things you might regret.

This is particularly an issue with print interviews, which, because they tend to be longer than live broadcast interviews, give the journalist so much more content from which to pick and choose. And of course any journalist is going to publish the most newsworthy comments a spokesperson makes, regardless of whether they do the spokesperson's organization more harm than good and regardless of whether the comments are representative of the interview as a whole.

In July 2000, Australia's Reconciliation Minister, Philip Ruddock, was interviewed by the *Washington Post* about the one-and-a-half billion dollars his government spent each year on social programmes for Aborigines. He was quoted in the article as saying: "But we are starting from a very low base. We're dealing with an indigenous population that had little contact with the rest of the world. We are dealing with people who were essentially hunter gatherers. They didn't have chariots. I don't think they invented the wheel."

Ruddock immediately came under fire from all sides for such an "insulting, demeaning view of Aboriginal culture", which, of course, is a highly sensitive topic in Australia.

Now Ruddock's defence was that the interview with the *Washington Post* had lasted for over an hour, and that he'd said quite a lot during that time that was, no doubt, culturally sensitive and sensible. Yet none of that was reported by the *Post*.

And therein lies the big danger of print interviews. You should never be too relaxed, because one loose, unwise comment in an hour-long interview might end up being the only thing that gets reported. No wonder so many spokespeople complain that "the journalist took my words out of context".

Ruddock survived that particular crisis and is still in government, but other public figures haven't been so lucky. Take football manager, Glenn Hoddle. In 1999, Hoddle, a committed Christian, was forced to resign as England's manager after being quoted by a national newspaper as saying that "disabled people are being punished for sins in a former life".

Hoddle later complained that his words had been "misconstrued, misunderstood and misinterpreted", and that they weren't even part of the formal interview (see section on "Off the record" in Chapter 7). But, once again, none of that necessarily matters to a journalist. If you say something newsworthy a print journalist will feel free to quote you even if that single quote is unrepresentative of your interview as a whole.

So even if you or your spokesperson have done hundreds of interviews, always be on your guard. Don't relax too much. Prepare for every interview as though it were your first. And say nothing that would damage you if it appeared as a headline on the front pages the next day. In a print interview, just as in a live broadcast interview, stick to your message. The more you stray from it, the more opportunity you give the journalist to quote you on something you wouldn't want reported.

Former Associated Press editor Michael Johnson says: "A journalist lives by only one ethical rule: to get the best, most surprising story he can tease you into delivering. He feels zero responsibility for the consequences to you. I once interviewed Alexander Solzhenitsyn in the full knowledge that my story would cause him more political problems. It never entered my mind to hold back. In fact I was eager to create the biggest noise possible. And I felt ethically justified. My guiding light was always 'the people's right to know'."

Over-confidence in recorded broadcast interviews

For most spokespeople, a recorded broadcast interview is less nerve-racking than a live interview. After all, if you lose your train of thought in a recorded interview, or suddenly get a frog in your throat, you'll be able to have another crack at it.

But just as you shouldn't relax too much in print interviews, nor should you do so in recorded broadcast interviews. Just as a print journalist can take your words out of context, so can the editors of recorded TV and radio programmes.

In 2009, the chief executive of the British Dental Association, Peter Ward, did a recorded TV interview with ITV's *Tonight* programme about mercury fillings. And it went horribly wrong. It seems that Ward was simply unprepared for the detailed questions he was being asked and either hadn't thought through his responses with enough care or wasn't expecting to be confronted by a journalist who was so well briefed.

This is how the interview went:

Reporter: Do you accept that mercury is a toxin?

Ward: Err, yes.

Reporter: Do you accept that it goes into our bodies and it is released from amalgam fillings?

Ward: Well, there is no real evidence that mercury causes any problems in that way.

Reporter: [reading from a document] The [unclear], their latest document says: "The largest source of mercury exposure for most people in developed countries is inhalation of mercury vapour from dental amalgam".

Ward:	Uh huh.
Reporter:	But you're saying it can't get into the body.
Ward:	Well, it says "exposure to mercury vapour", and mercury vapour . . . while you're having fillings done obviously there's mercury vapour around. What I'm saying to you is that the long-lasting, remaining residues of mercury aren't shown to be present in people's bodies.
Reporter:	Right but the actual vapour coming off the mercury filling . . .
Ward:	At the time of placement.
Reporter:	. . . using the BDA situation, that can only happen when the filling is put in or the filling is removed.
Ward:	Yeah.
Reporter:	So it can't happen when you brush. It can't happen when you chew.
Ward:	That's right. But you've got to look at the quantities involved here and the significance of, of . . .
Reporter:	Yes but you just told me it was zero.
Ward:	[laughs] Okay.

At this point Ward throws up his hands and waves them above his head smiling and saying "Lalalalalala" and then grins at the journalist. We can only assume that Ward knew the interview was going badly wrong and was trying to stop it being broadcast by deliberately ruining the shot. The dialogue then continued.

Reporter:	Is it zero or not?
Ward:	No I'm not going to do this. If you're going to try and trap me I'm not doing it.
Reporter:	I'm not trapping you. You told me that there was no . . . that there was no mercury vapour released from an amalgam filling.
Ward:	No, I'm not doing this.
Reporter:	Not doing what? Answering the questions we told you we were going to ask you?

Ward:	[still smiling] You didn't tell me you were going to do it that way.
Reporter:	Do what, what way? I told you it was going to be about amalgam fillings. That's what we're talking about, the safety of amalgam fillings. [Ward looks away for a few moments, and then back to the reporter.] And your answer is?
Ward:	No, I'll answer your serious questions if you're going to ask me . . .
Reporter:	That is a serious question.
Ward:	No, alright, okay.

At this point Ward approaches the camera and starts waving into the lens with both hands. Again, we can only assume he did this in an attempt to ruin the pictures so that they could never be broadcast.

The trouble is, they were.

This interview is painful to watch (if you can bear to, Google: "Peter Ward British Dental Association") and it's difficult not to feel sorry for Ward, and alarmed at how this smart, impressive-looking executive could emotionally unravel to quite such an extent within a few seconds.

Following the broadcast Ward wrote an "open apology to all dentists" on the BDA website, including these words: "The scenes that were broadcast represent a small fraction of the interview that did not follow the sequence I expected and caught me by surprise. That is, however, no excuse for the spoiling tactics I adopted on the spur of the moment . . . The interviewer was with me for approximately one hour, during which time I answered many questions . . ."

So just as Australian minister Philip Ruddock was alarmed that one short segment of his interview – the worst from his point of view – could be published by the *Washington Post*, so Peter Ward was horrified that the most embarrassing segment of his hour-long TV interview would be the bit that the producers chose to broadcast.

The lesson for the rest of us is simple: prepare, prepare and prepare, particularly for an issues-based interview of the sort Peter Ward was facing. Don't relax too much. And don't assume that the journalist won't have done plenty of preparation too.

What's better: live or recorded?

If you have the confidence to go live, then go live. Yes, you only have one go at it in a live interview. And yes, it can get the heart racing. But if it goes out live, your words cannot be taken out of context.

Summary

1 Keep a positive mindset by remembering that the journalist usually wants you to perform well . . .

2 . . . and reminding yourself that you are the expert.

3 Do some practice interviews to flush out the messages that need changing.

4 Do some voice exercises to make sure you speak fluently . . .

5 . . . and some breathing exercises to release any tension.

6 In a print or recorded broadcast interview, particularly, be careful not to say anything that, taken in isolation, could be harmful to you or your organization.

7 In all interviews, make sure that your messages, examples and evidence stand up to scrutiny from a well-prepared journalist.

8 Keep any anger well under control, and instead use assertiveness and passion.

9 If you're given the choice between a live and recorded broadcast interview, take the live option

Exercises

Imagine the most stressful media interview you could be involved in for your organization.

1 Using the techniques in this chapter, how might you ensure that you go into the interview with a confident mindset?

2 What sort of voice and breathing exercises would work for you?

3 What sort of statements might you be tempted to make that might damage you or your organization?

4 How can you ensure you'll keep your cool regardless of the provocation?

5 What are the most challenging questions you could be asked, and how might you respond?

Voice and body language

05

In every media training session I've ever conducted, the vital role of voice and body language quickly becomes apparent to delegates. Nearly always, having completed their first set of interviews and seen them played back on video, delegates comment first on the non-verbal elements of their interview, such as vocal fluency, facial expressions, gestures, eye contact and pace of delivery. Only then do they refer to the content of the interview and the way questions were answered.

This focus on voice and body language first, and content second, is entirely consistent with research conducted in 2011 by two US academics, David Neal and Tanya Chartrand, into how people recognize the emotions others are feeling. Their research confirmed that whatever a speaker experiences physically (such as elation, panic or boredom) the audience *also* experiences *on a physical, emotional and often conscious level*. They do so because they "automatically mimic the expressions" displayed on the speaker's face.

This means that you or your spokesperson must not rely on content alone to communicate. You must communicate physically too. If you tell the audience that you are excited, but look and sound bored to tears, the audience will also feel bored to tears and will assume you are too. Likewise, you might say in a TV interview: "Our company is committed to maintaining a factory in this town." That message will be believed by the viewers if your voice and body language are consistent with it. However, if you convey uncertain body language (eg poor eye contact) and a lack of vocal conviction (eg mumbling and hesitancy), people are more likely to trust the non-verbal signals than the verbal ones.

Effective and meaningful communication therefore requires words to be accompanied by *congruent* voice and body language. And there are three absolute essentials to good, strong voice and body language:

- Eye contact;
- Posture;
- Pace of delivery.

Without these three elements it is difficult, if not impossible, to communicate a message well. Of course, these three elements are particularly important in a TV interview (and pace of delivery in a radio interview). But they are also essential to good communication in a face-to-face interview with a print journalist.

Eye contact

Eye contact with the journalist (not, in a TV interview, with the camera) is the single biggest element of good body language. If a spokesperson cannot look at the journalist in the eye – and it will be obvious not just to the journalist but to viewers as well – then nothing they say will be believed. Simply, a spokesperson with poor eye contact risks coming across as shifty and untrustworthy.

Some people find prolonged eye contact with a journalist difficult to maintain. It gives them a kind of burning sensation, and they feel a strong temptation to look away. If this happens to you or your spokesperson, try to focus on the bridge of the journalist's nose, their mouth, or both alternately. To the journalist, and to the viewers, it will appear exactly as though you are looking straight at the journalist's eyes, but you won't suffer that uncomfortable burning sensation.

In the May 2007 edition of *Tactics* magazine, Brad Phillips, president of Phillips Media Relations, gave some excellent advice about eye contact in media interviews: "The ability to maintain direct eye contact is a critical skill. The failure to do so makes a spokesperson look nervous at best and shifty at worst. Strong eye contact signals intensity – yet another way to communicate passion." And former CBS Chicago anchorman Antonia Mora was quoted in *Corporate Legal*

Times (Flahardy, 2004) as saying: "Look at the reporter in the eye and act as though they're the only person in the world you want to be with."

The message is simple: eye contact is vital.

"Down-the-line" interviews

There is one exception to the never-look-at-the-camera rule, and that's when you do a down-the-line TV interview. In down-the-line interviews you and the journalist are in different locations, and while the journalist and viewers can see and hear you, you can usually only hear the journalist through an earpiece.

This type of interview is often regarded as the most difficult of all, as you must look straight into the lens of the camera or, more frequently these days, into the camera on your computer for a live interview over Skype. It feels like an unnatural thing to do, so you must try to ignore all distractions around you, such as bright lights, technicians moving around and cramped conditions, as you focus on the camera. You might even try to imagine a friendly member of the audience looking back at you. (For a Skype interview, remember where the camera is on your computer and look straight at it, not to the middle of the screen.)

Former TV reporter Shirley Brice had this to say about down-the-line interviews in *Tactics* magazine (May 2003): "Remember, it's only a conversation. Try to focus on this point before the interview begins. There are plenty of mechanics to deal with in a live remote, but the bottom line is that the audience only sees it as a conversation. Keep your focus constantly on the camera lens, even when you think the interview is over. You'll get the 'all clear' from the producer when it's safe to look away. If you need a break during the interview, look down and slightly to the side. In the training business, this is called a reflective glance down and it's something we all do in normal conversation.

"If you've got a fellow guest who interrupts, stand your ground and politely say, 'I want to finish my point'. Some interviewees and hosts will try to control the interview by interrupting. Do your homework. To avoid surprises, pump the producer or booker prior to the show for a general outline of the interview. They probably won't give you specific questions but should provide general parameters ... Mistakes? No big deal. Everyone makes mistakes in normal conversation. If you find yourself stumbling on air, slow down and let those mistakes roll off. Don't beat yourself up. There's an old broadcast expression, 'Television is not brain surgery'."

Posture

Imagine you're watching a spokesperson doing an interview on television. Throughout the interview, the spokesperson is:

- Leaning away from the journalist;
- Rocking backwards and forwards;
- Rolling their head from side to side.

As a viewer you'll no doubt be completely distracted and unable to concentrate on what the spokesperson is saying. And even if you were able to concentrate on the message, would you believe it? Probably not.

A good posture is vital to strong body language. It sounds simple, but remarkably enough this basic requirement can be difficult to achieve under pressure, particularly in a studio environment. Interviewees sway from side to side, rock backwards and forwards, lean to one side or jerk forward – always unconsciously. (That's just one reason why media training can be so useful, as it allows us to see ourselves as others see us.)

For stand-up interviews there are two ways to ensure a straight posture:

1 Place your feet according to the width of your shoulders, or slightly further apart, and then spread your weight evenly between them. Try to have a little bit of "give" in your knees, so that you are not ramrod straight, but relaxed straight. You have now adopted what presentation trainers call "the centred position".

2 Put most of your weight on one foot (I, for example, am more comfortable with most of my weight on my left foot) and then use the other foot simply to keep your balance.

Both of these techniques will allow you to maintain a straight head and shoulders, while still being relaxed and comfortable. You then avoid the dreaded shifting of weight from foot to foot and swaying from side to side, which can be so distracting for TV viewers.

Sit-down interviews

In the world of media training, BBC stands for "Bum in Back of Chair". In other words, sit up straight, show the journalist that you want to be there and that you are engaged in the whole process. If there is a table or desk right in front of you, place your hands on the table. If you want to cross your legs, that's okay, but just make sure that your shoulders don't get too hunched.

Is that all there is to it? Not quite, because there are still adjustments you can make to enhance your presence. The former leader of Britain's Labour Party, Ed Miliband, is a good example of this. Throughout the early years of his leadership of the party Miliband had what some people unkindly called "an image problem". In short, his critics believed he looked too weak, young and callow – and even geeky – to be prime minister (even though he's well over 40). Miliband's media interviews seemed to confirm this impression.

However, by the end of 2014, having hired new media trainers, Miliband had made a subtle but noticeable change to his posture for TV interviews, which had a big impact on his TV image. He simply took up more space. He spread his shoulders, opened his legs a little and used wider gestures. These small changes made him look much more at ease with himself, impressive and statesmanlike.

So someone regarded as weak can project greater strength, just as Miliband did, simply by taking up more space. In their book *Compelling People*, John Neffinger and Matthew Kohut describe how strong people "make themselves at home anywhere, occupy a lot of space and move about freely rather than getting locked in one space. Above all, they exert control over space, making it clear who is in charge . . . Good upright posture projects strength . . . Standing tall demonstrates confidence."

There is no doubt that the subtle changes Miliband made to his posture – taking up more space – allowed him to project more strength to the viewers.

In contrast to Miliband, Prime Minister David Cameron has rarely been regarded as weak. In fact, if anything, his critics claim they can see an arrogance and sense of entitlement in him. So taking up more space in that way would hold no advantage for Cameron. He is well served by taking a more conventional posture of (very slightly) leaning in towards the journalist and keeping his legs closer together.

Good posture gives the spokesperson more confidence

A strong, upright posture not only makes a spokesperson *look* strong and confident, but also makes them *feel* strong and confident.

There have been many occasions when I have faced nervous interviewees on camera who have felt much more commanding and in control once they simply stand up straight and tall. Of course they can also stand up straight and tall, or sit up straight and tall, in the moments before they go into their interview, giving them a timely confidence boost. And once the interview starts, adopting that strong, upright posture eases the tension and gives reassurance during those first few vital moments of the interview.

Phone interviews

Many spokespeople are tasked with doing interviews over the phone with print journalists. It would be logical to assume that body language is irrelevant in such circumstances. However, to ensure that their voices carry maximum authority, phone interviewees should consider *standing up* to do their interviews. Typically, a voice carries more energy, passion and resonance when a person is standing up, and they feel more commanding and confident as a result.

Pace of delivery

The perfect pace of delivery varies from person to person, and indeed from culture to culture. Nelson Mandela, for example, had a wonderfully measured pace of delivery, and he always held the attention of his audience. In contrast, political leaders in Britain tend to go at a faster clip.

However, it is possible to go *too* quickly and *too* slowly. Either way, you are in danger of losing the connection with your audience.

Speaking too quickly

Some of my trainees, particularly those from northern European countries, simply speak too quickly. In extreme cases, they gabble, so that even if the audience hears every word they simply don't have time to compute it all. To the listener it feels like they're drinking from a power hose – and the message simply gets lost. Even worse, a spokesperson who speaks too quickly gives the impression of wanting the interview to be over as soon as possible, and therefore of being unsure of themselves and uncertain of their content.

Less is more in media interviews. It is far better to communicate one or two messages well than to gabble through three and do none of them justice. The listeners don't want the interview to be a stressful, rushed experience. They want to receive messages in bite-sized chunks. Journalists too want you to slow down, especially print journalists who may be taking lots of notes as you speak (if you're interesting enough). So don't go so fast that they simply can't keep up with you. That's a recipe for being misquoted.

For spokespeople who have a natural tendency to go too quickly, the solution is to introduce pauses. Pausing not only gives the listeners time to compute and react to what's been said, but it gives them much more confidence in the spokesperson, because it shows that they are on top of their brief. Pausing is particularly important after a spokesperson has communicated a key message. It has the effect of highlighting and signposting that key message, making it stand out from the rest of the interview.

Communications expert and presentation trainer Andrew Tidmarsh offers this advice: "Shape the thought before you speak. This results in speech that drives the thought through to the end without interruption. It is the repetitions, hesitations and discourse markers that interrupt the flow and discourage the listener from receiving the information. Few people can process and speak at the same time. Most of us need a moment to breathe, think and then speak. A pause to breathe and think is less disruptive than most people think. We are generally tolerant of giving people space and time to gather their thoughts. The overall aim is to speak with clarity. This involves delivering each thought as complete actions one at a time. As a trend, our speech is becoming increasingly fractured and 'telegrammatic'. I encourage a new habit: speaking in complete uninterrupted sentences."

Going too slowly

The adrenaline surge that spokespeople get when doing broadcast interviews tends to make them speak too quickly. However, just occasionally spokespeople go too slowly.

In my experience of training people from all over the world, delegates from sub-Saharan Africa, of both genders, often have the richest, most measured and rounded delivery. This is generally something that works in their favour, as they are easy and comforting to listen too. But on occasions a very measured, soothing pace of delivery can lull and relax the listener so much that the content no longer gets through.

This is where a bit more energy and spark is needed. The spokesperson needs to imagine that the audience is *literally falling asleep*, and their job is to keep the audience awake with a more lively and energized delivery. It's entirely possible. Think of South Africa's Bishop Desmond Tutu. For sure, he speaks quite slowly, but he does so with unbeatable energy and enthusiasm.

Other aspects of good voice and body language

Gestures

Many people like to talk with their hands (I am one of them), and feel that they can't communicate properly unless they do so. The good news for such people is that gestures are perfectly acceptable in TV interviews, so long as:

- They are strong and deliberate (limp-wrist hand gestures undermine a strong message);
- They aren't so excessive that it looks like the spokesperson is conducting an orchestra, with heaving shoulders and swinging arms.

In short, don't make your gestures distract from your message. Your gestures should be firm yet relaxed, supporting the overall impression of a spokesperson who is alert but at ease.

Smiling

Some people, like former British prime minister Tony Blair, have a natural smile, even when their face is in a "resting position". Others, like Blair's successor Prime Minister Gordon Brown, do not.

There's no doubt that the Blairs of this world have an advantage over the Browns when it comes to public performances of any sort, including media interviews. People tend to warm to a natural smile, seeing the person who wears it as more likeable and easier to do business with.

So what can be done for the person who doesn't have a natural smile? The first thing is not to force it, because a forced smile comes across as fake and insincere. Gordon Brown found this to his cost when he tried forcing himself to smile during a YouTube presentation [Google "Gordon Brown smiles YouTube"]. As you'll see, a forced, fake smile can be worse than no smile at all.

People smile not just with their mouths, but with their eyes too, and a genuine smile lights up the whole face. Therefore the only way to smile *genuinely* is to *genuinely* feel the emotions that make us smile. So when I train people whose natural resting face is rather dour and serious, I ask them to imagine themselves, just before the interview starts, in a place they love to be – such as on holiday with a loved one sharing a glass of wine as the sun sets over a gorgeous view. That memory lifts the face into a natural smile and is much more effective than forcing one's mouth into a fake smile.

Vocal modulation

Some voices are more melodious and expressive than others, and therefore more interesting to listen to. The result? The message is far more likely to be listened to and acted upon.

A spokesperson I always admire for his wonderfully expressive tone of voice is the UK personal finance expert Martin Lewis. It's no surprise that the media love to interview him, because he speaks with such energy and vigour, giving the impression that communicating his message in that interview is the only thing he cares about at that time. And I've no doubt it is. As a result, Lewis gives broadcasters exactly what they want. To see and hear him in action, Google "Martin Lewis personal finance interview".

In contrast, we've all seen and heard spokespeople whose voices are timid, flat and monotonous, and some are capable of making the most interesting subjects thoroughly boring.

As with smiling, it is difficult to force yourself to be expressive, and to will your voice to be well modulated and resonant. Try to do so and you just come across as fake and insincere. So, just as with a genuine smile, the only way to be *genuinely* expressive is to be *genuinely* enthused by your message. The audience is never going to be more enthusiastic about your message than you are. So think to yourself as you prepare for your interview about *why* the message is important, *what* it can do for people, and *how* it can improve their lives.

If you believe in your message, if you feel a genuine connection to it, then your voice will naturally become more expressive and modulated.

Erms, errs and you knows

One of the things that some people often don't realize they do, until they hear a recording of their voice, is that they use filler sounds and words such as:

- Erm
- Err
- Uh

- You know
- Kind of
- Sort of

The odd filler word is fine and sounds completely natural. But in extreme cases some spokespeople use these filler sounds several times in every sentence, which can be irritating and distracting for viewers and listeners, and give the impression of someone who is simply not up to the job of representing their organization.

There are two reasons why people use filler words:

1 They feel the need to fill silence with sound, even though it can be counter-productive. There is no magic solution to this. They just need consciously to listen to themselves speak, in every-day conversations with family, friends and colleagues, and practise pausing rather than filling the silence with a filler sound. It can be done. David Beckham, for example, has improved the fluency of his delivery dramatically over the last decade. Sure, he still says "umm" and "you know" more than he might like, but his improvement has been outstanding.

2 They are genuinely unsure of their content. For example, the leader of Britain's Green Party, Natalie Bennett, was almost left lost for words as she tried to explain the financial implications of her Party's housing policy on LBC Radio in February 2015. This is how part of the interview went:

Presenter: The third key theme is "The Greens will ensure everyone has a secure, affordable place to live". How would that be brought about?

Bennett: A couple of things that we want to focus on. In terms of council housing, we want to build 500,000 new social rent homes.

Presenter: Good lord, where would you get the money from for that?

Bennett: Well, what we want to do is fund that particularly by removing tax relief on mortgage interests for private landlords. We have a situation where . . .

Presenter:	How much would that bring in?
Bennett:	Private landlords at the moment are basically running away with the situation of hugely rising rents while collecting huge amounts of housing benefit.
Presenter:	How much would that be worth, the mortgage relief for private landlords?
Bennett:	Erm . . . well . . . it's . . . that's part of the whole costing.
Presenter:	Yes, but how much would that bring? The cost of 500,000 homes, let's start with that. How much would that be?
Bennett:	Right, well, that's, erm . . . you've got a total cost . . . erm . . . that we're . . . that will be spelt out in our manifesto.
Presenter:	So you don't know?
Bennett:	No, well, err.
Presenter:	You don't, ok. So you don't know how much those homes are going to cost, but the way it's going to be funded is mortgage relief from private landlords. How much is that worth?
Bennett:	Right, well what we're looking at with the figures here. Erm, what we need to do is actually . . . uh . . . we're looking at a total spend of £2.7 . . . billion.
Presenter:	500,000 homes, £2.7 billion? What are they made of, plywood?
Bennett:	Erm, basically what we're talking about is 500,000 new homes and basically each one pound spent on this brings back £2.40 . . .
Presenter:	Yes, but what is the total cost of 500,000 homes?
Bennett:	[Long, long pause] Erm . . . it's a cost of £60,000 per home.
Presenter:	£60,000 per home?
Bennett:	Because what we're talking about is, is the opportunity for . . .
Presenter:	That can't include the land?
Bennett:	Well, what we're talking about is, what we want to see is the possibility of, um, of homes being built . . .

Presenter:	That's not much more than a large conservatory, £60,000. So where's the land, how are you going to pay for the land?
Bennett:	[Even longer pause] Right, well, what we're, what we're looking at doing is, is . . . is basically [cough, cough, cough] . . .
Presenter:	Are you alright?
Bennett:	Yes, sorry, as you can probably hear, I have got a huge cold.
Presenter:	I'm terribly sorry to hear that.
Bennett:	So, so what we need to do is, is social rental homes.
Presenter:	Right. Still don't see how you're going to get this . . . some at £60,000 . . . you don't actually know how much this is going to cost, do you?
Bennett:	Uh, yes, we've got a fully-costed programme which we'll be releasing, which will be released . . .
Presenter:	Shouldn't you be aware of what that cost will be now?
Bennett:	Uh, right, yes. So what we're talking about is £6 billion per year. So the current budget is £1.5 billion a year.
Presenter:	£6 billion? That will be attained by taking mortgage relief from private landlords? That's £6 billion-worth is it?
Bennett:	And we're also looking at investing . . . [long pause]. Yes, well, it's . . . we've got the fully costed figures here.
Presenter:	You've said that on a couple of occasions. How much does mortgage relief from private landlords bring in then?
Bennett:	[Long pause, cough, cough] Basically, we're talking about an overall saving of £4.5 billion.
Presenter:	What? Mortgage relief is worth £4.5 billion a year?
Bennett:	And this is other saving as well, from private landlords as well, we're looking at housing benefit reforms and what we also want to do is bring in caps on private tenants.

Presenter:	Yes, do you think you could have perhaps have ginned up on this a bit more Natalie Bennett?
Bennett:	[Cough, cough] Uh, I think that we're talking about a whole range of . . .
Presenter:	No, you personally, do you think you might have ginned up a little, might you have read into this a little more in hindsight?

Bennett later apologized to Green Party members for what she admitted was an "absolutely excruciating performance" caused by a "mind blank". But, more likely, Bennett just hadn't prepared herself well enough for the sort of questioning that any good journalist would adopt. The presenter's questions weren't in any way devious, unfair or particularly aggressive. Bennett simply wasn't briefed well enough, and her excruciating use of filler words was the result.

We discussed in Chapter 2 the importance of preparing thoroughly for a media interview – particularly a live broadcast interview, when you need to get it right first time. Preparation means being on top of your brief, and it means predicting the sort of questions any good journalist will ask.

Using notes

In Chapter 3 we discussed the ideal set of notes for a media interview – something simple and manageable, all on one sheet. Notes are highly effective in a print or radio interview, where the spokesperson cannot be seen by the audience. You or your spokesperson can glance down at your notes throughout your interview, reminding yourself that you need to bridge into your key messages and make them dominate the agenda for the interview as a whole.

But in any kind of TV interview, including video podcasts, using notes will undermine your credibility and make you look unsure of your content. So you must memorize your messages, examples and evidence.

This is what makes TV and video interviews more difficult than any other. I've lost count of the number of times I've interviewed people, some very senior, who forget their key messages the moment the interview starts. They simply answer the questions that are put to them.

The only way to overcome this is to practise your interview until you know your messages, examples and evidence so thoroughly that you can bridge into them at will, whatever question you might be asked. An interview is a great opportunity to communicate to your chosen audience. So don't waste that opportunity by not taking it seriously enough. Practise, practise and practise some more.

Nervous ticks

Nervous ticks of various sorts can easily distract TV viewers. They include:

- Constantly sweeping away your hair fringe;
- Clasping and unclasping your hands;
- Biting your lip;
- Playing with a ring on your finger.

These movements are usually unconscious and caused by the adrenaline that pumps through us when we're nervous, creating energy that our bodies feel the need to release. But they come across to viewers and listeners as anxiety and a lack of control, which leaves them unable to concentrate on the message.

Some spokespeople are able to control these nervous movements as soon as they become aware of them. Others need to find an alternative way of releasing the pent-up nervous energy – and the best way is through firm, deliberate gestures.

Dress sense

What should you wear for a TV or video interview? There are three factors that can help you decide:

1 What makes you feel comfortable? A TV interview is stressful enough without feeling awkward and uncomfortable about

what you're wearing. So if you never normally wear a tie it might be best not to wear one for the first time in years on a live TV programme.

2 What best reflects your organization's brand? For example, if you are the spokesperson for a major international bank, the viewers might expect you to wear a business suit. However, if you represent a wildlife charity, you might prefer something more casual.

3 What will the person interviewing you be wearing? If you're being interviewed on a business programme in a studio on national TV, it's likely that the presenters will be wearing business suits – so you might want to do the same. However, if you're being interviewed as part of an outside broadcast in the middle of an industrial estate, you might follow the journalist's lead and wear something more informal.

Other things to bear in mind:

1 If you're being interviewed in a TV studio, you will almost certainly be offered make up before you go on air. Take it. The presenters will be wearing it and if you don't you're in danger of looking washed out.

2 Try not to wear things that will distract the viewers' attention from your message, such as dangly earrings or loud ties.

Former LBC and BBC presenter Gill Pyrah says: "I took three outfits to my first TV job, thinking that a choice, depending on the report I would be doing, would be helpful. But all the clothes were black and/or white, which can be tricky to light well, so the director was furiously unimpressed. But better that than fussy patterns or bright red, which can look hectic, as most people have their TVs tuned to be much more densely coloured than is true to life.

"Strappy shoulders, big jewellery and low necklines are disastrous if you want to be taken seriously. Otherwise for women: check you can sit in a tight skirt without having to tug at it to cover your crotch; and don't wear heels so high you'll wobble if you're asked to stand or walk.

"Leave time to have a mirror check. I did some training with one very competent and successful CEO several times, and her messaging was great, yet her PR team wanted to book her in for another session. When I asked why, they said: 'We can't get her to comb her hair and we need you to tell her it's actually important, not frivolous. What she says is great but it's missed because viewers don't see past her hair.' Which is sad but still true."

Specialist media-training cameraman, Nigel Blackman, adds: "On high-definition TV, which more and more people are getting these days, images can actually look too sharp if a spokesman wears bright coloured checks or stripes. The effect gets amplified and the clothing looks more dominant then the spokesperson's face. Darker, natural and pastel shades are always safer."

Summary

1 The three most important elements of good voice and body language are eye contact, posture and pace of delivery.

2 In a TV or video interview, eye contact should be with the journalist, not the camera . . .

3 . . . except in a "down-the-line" interview, when you should look straight into the lens.

4 A good posture means a straight head and shoulders with no shifting of weight from side to side.

5 People who tend to talk too fast should try to introduce pauses into their delivery.

6 Gestures should be firm and deliberate, rather than jittery or limp-wrsted.

7 A forced smile is worse than no smile at all.

8 Good vocal modulation results from being genuinely passionate about your subject.

9 Eradicate erms, uhs and other filler words by practising pausing in everyday speech.

10 For a TV interview, the primary consideration when deciding what to wear is to think what you'll be comfortable in.

Exercises

1 Practise doing a "down-the-line" interview by looking straight into the camera on your computer.

2 Find out your best posture for doing a stand-up interview by trying out the two main alternatives outlined in this chapter.

3 Record yourself speaking. Is your pace about right, or do you tend to go too quickly (or slowly)?

4 Video yourself doing a practice interview. Are your gestures firm yet relaxed? . . .

5 . . . Do you have a natural smile? . . .

6 . . . And do you have a natural expressiveness and vocal modulation?

The perfect tone of voice

06

In any interview that you or your spokesperson carries out you are in control of two things: what you say and how you say it. The latter, in turn, comprises two areas: your body language and pace of delivery, which we discussed in Chapter 5, and your tone of voice, which we discuss in this chapter.

However enthralling your message, you won't inspire your audience to action unless you communicate it in an equally compelling tone of voice. As Gary Hudson and Sarah Rowlands write in *The Broadcast Journalism Handbook*: "Often the emotional impact of an interview will be the most important element."

A W.I.S.E. tone

The perfect tone of voice for any interview is W.I.S.E.:

Warm

Intelligent

Sincere

Enthusiastic/Empathetic

Most spokespeople find it easier to convey intelligence and sincerity than warmth, enthusiasm and empathy.

Warm

See "Warm, enthusiastic and empathetic" on page 105.

Intelligent

Intelligence, in a media interview, is not about demonstrating a high IQ. It's about speaking sensibly, knowledgeably and authoritatively on the subject at hand.

Most organizations are only too aware that their spokespeople must have the required knowledge and intelligence about the subject of the interview, so this is rarely a problem. However, it *can* be a problem if the lead spokesperson in a particular area suddenly becomes unavailable, and someone without the required knowledge has to step in at the last minute. That stand-in spokesperson might have the highest IQ, but if they don't have enough knowledge they risk coming across as unintelligent about the subject being discussed.

Public-relations executives can face this difficulty if they are tasked with acting as spokespeople for their organization, often having to communicate about a wide range of detailed, technical subjects. They need to get up to speed quickly, or they risk being found out live in the interview. That's why, in general, public-relations people often prefer to brief and support the spokesperson rather than to act as the spokesperson themselves. US branding consultancy, Studiothing, writes: "There are certainly instances where the spokesperson is not available, and only in those cases – where all other spokespeople are exhausted – should the PR person step in . . ."

Sincere

This is about communicating openly and honestly. If there is one element of W.I.S.E. that is more important than any other, this is it, because *in*sincerity can actually turn your audience against you.

The old joke (usually attributed to American actor George Burns) is that if you can fake sincerity, you've got it made. Well, that may be true. But it's very difficult to fake sincerity, and its absence is a recipe for disaster. So don't even try to fake it. Instead, feel it.

Over the last decade or so, I've trained and interviewed many thousands of spokespeople for many hundreds of organizations, and I'm pleased to report that nearly all of them have come across as entirely sincere. In general, they *do* want to communicate openly and honestly; they *believe* in what they say; and if their organization has been at fault, they've held their hands up and *admitted* it.

Only a handful of them have come across as insincere, and when they have done so, it is nearly always because they have:

1 Lied. It's not just that you might be found out one day, but that most people lie badly, making it obvious they don't believe a word they're saying (see section on Chris Huhne in Chapter 7).

2 Denied fault (see Chapter 9).

3 Avoided the question (see Chapter 7).

4 Articulated what sounds like a strong and impressive message but have then been utterly incapable of backing it up with any examples or evidence. The message therefore appears empty, and the messenger appears insincere.

Quite simply, if you or your spokesperson don't believe in the message yourself, if you don't have examples and evidence to back it up, don't try to communicate it. If someone else in the organization asks you to communicate a message, you must insist on having examples and evidence to support it. If nothing is supplied don't communicate that message in the interview because it will be exposed as empty under the slightest prodding from the journalist.

For instance, imagine you're a spokesperson for a leading car manufacturer, and your key message is that your cars are the safest on the roads. To back up that message, and to show that you and your organization are sincere, you'll need one or more of these:

- Examples of safety awards that you've won;
- Safety test results from independent and authoritative assessors;
- Examples of safety features that your cars come with that other cars don't;
- Quotes about safety from people who have bought your cars.

Warm, enthusiastic and empathetic

Warmth helps you communicate in any type of interview; enthusiasm helps you in a promotional interview; and empathy supports you in a crisis interview. In an issues-based interview, you need a bit of all three.

Some people are lucky and have an authentically warm, empathetic and/or enthusiastic style. For example, we spoke in Chapter 5 about how some people have a melodious, well-modulated voice, which is always easier on the ear than something flat and monotonous.

However, most spokespeople find it a challenge to convey warmth, empathy and enthusiasm. And it's understandable that they should, because giving a media interview, especially when you're new to it, can be an uncomfortable experience. In some cases, you'll be in an unfamiliar setting, such as a studio, with lights and camera pointing straight at you. In others you'll be asked searching and even hostile questions from a journalist who doesn't care whether the final news story is good or bad from your point of view. And in all cases you'll lack complete control over the end product – which is the very nature of a media interview and which makes it such a great opportunity but also a threat when you get it wrong.

So it is entirely understandable that you or your spokesperson will feel uncomfortable in a media interview. But the problem with feeling uncomfortable is that it tends to shut down warmth, enthusiasm and empathy, even for those who are, when they are feeling comfortable and relaxed, the most naturally warm, enthusiastic and empathetic people imaginable.

People who are normally the life and soul of the party can clam up completely when a camera is pointed at them. As the BBC's Jeremy Vine says (reported in *The Broadcast Journalism Handbook*): "I do think that as professional broadcasters we underestimate the extent to which coming into a studio and talking to somebody and having five minutes to say your bit . . . we underestimate how frightening that is." Even if you're speaking to a print journalist over the phone, it can still be an uncomfortable experience for someone who's not used to it.

So the big question for anyone doing a media interview, broadcast or print, is this: how do you convey warmth, enthusiasm and empathy through your tone of voice *even when you're feeling uncomfortable*?

Well, the good news is that you don't have to put on an act, pretend to be something you're not or try to change your personality – all of which would, in any case, be counter-productive and make you come across as insincere. All you need to do is:

1 Keep your delivery as conversational as possible;
2 Use mind pictures.

1 Keeping your delivery as conversational as possible

If you or your spokesperson is doing a broadcast interview for a general audience you will be well advised to imagine that audience to be made up of intelligent 14-year-olds. In fact, that's the advice that TV producers will sometimes give spokespeople who are about to do an interview aimed at a general audience.

Economist Daniel S Hamermesh offers similar advice. Writing for his fellow economists about doing media interviews in the *Journal of Economic Education* (2004), he says: "Economists should speak in a language that their high-school graduate nephew of above-average intelligence can understand."

This applies to print interviews too. After all, if you give a jargon-filled interview to a print journalist they will have to "translate" your jargon for their readers, and will very possibly get it wrong.

So cut out the jargon, slice through the long complicated words and the corporate-speak, and try to find conversational alternatives instead. Ask yourself, if I really were communicating with a room full of intelligent 14-year-olds, what terminology would I use, what language would I adopt and what tone of voice would I convey? Do that successfully, and you'll probably have the right tone for a general audience.

It sounds easy. But in practice it can be quite hard for some spokespeople to speak conversationally when they are used to using the jargon and corporate-speak that is common currency in their organization and industry.

One of my favourite media-interview clips is of an educational expert talking about the importance of school pupils staying at school after the age of 16. This is one of her answers, and the words and phrases in italics are examples of jargon and/or corporate-speak:

"I think it's important that students stay on at school *post-16* really for three main reasons. Firstly, students today can expect to have five different careers in their lifetime such are *the dynamics of the workplace* in terms of both technological change and in terms of working practices. Students need to have a breadth of qualifications that will equip them to meet these changes and also an attitude to study that will equip them for *life-long learning* should they need to add to these qualifications at a later stage. Secondly I think that students *post-16* develop *higher-order thinking skills*. Most students develop the ability for *abstract, conceptual thought* and I think academic study *facilitates* this. To enter the higher-paid professions such as medical, legal and perhaps corporate management this *capacity* for *higher-level thinking skills* is essential. And finally, *earning capacity*. Over 70 per cent of our sixth formers enter and complete university degree courses, and research has shown that graduates can earn *in excess of* 40 per cent more than *non-graduates*."

Each of these unconversational words and phrases could easily be replaced by something more everyday:

Jargon	Everyday
post-16	after the age of 16/after 16/from 16 onwards
the dynamics of the workplace	the changes to working life
life-long learning	continuing to learn and develop throughout their life
higher-order thinking skills	an ability to analyse problems and complex ideas (NB I'm guessing that's what it means)
abstract, conceptual thought	the ability to analyse things
facilitates	helps develop
capacity	ability
earning capacity	how much they will earn
in excess of	more than
non-graduates	people who don't go to university

Now, of course, some of these examples of corporate-speak are worse than others. Some people might not understand the term "higher-order thinking skills" at all, or might only have a vague notion of what it means, whereas the words "in excess of" are easy to translate into something more conversational. But even these relatively-easy-to-translate terms, when taken together in quick succession, give the impression not of a real human being, with natural warmth, enthusiasm and empathy, but of a robot reading out a section of a report. Each little piece of corporate-speak or jargon serves to raise a barrier between the interviewee and the viewers or listeners. And it's really hard to convey warmth through a barrier.

In contrast, this is the more conversational language that the educational expert could have used:

"I think there are three reasons why pupils should stay on at school after 16. First, they need to get a good broad set of qualifications, and that's particularly important these days given the changes that are taking place to working life. In fact, experts predict that many of today's school pupils will end up having five completely different careers in their lifetime. So a broad set of qualifications will help them hugely as they go through their careers. Secondly, after the age of 16 pupils start to think in a different and much more advanced way, which is essential if they're going to aim for professions such as medicine, the law and corporate management. And finally, pupils who stay at school after 16 and go on to university tend to earn more. In fact, the latest research shows that they can earn at least 40 per cent more than people who don't go to university."

Many spokespeople think that by using long words, jargon and corporate-speak they will come across as more intelligent, knowledgeable and authoritative. But they don't. They just come across as inaccessible and cold.

A case in point is a former trainee of mine, an ecology expert. At the start of our training session together she told me how horrified she was at the result of a recorded BBC TV interview she had given a few days earlier, aimed at a general audience. As is the nature of recorded TV, her interview had lasted about half an hour, in which she had spoken knowledgeably and authoritatively about her subject. And yet, the only bit of her interview that was actually broadcast was her description of voles as being "like little fat hairy men plopping into the water". She was amazed that the producers had chosen that line as the bit to broadcast, and mortified because she thought that such a seemingly childish description would undermine her authority and professionalism.

Well, there are two things to say about that. First, it shouldn't surprise anyone that the broadcasters decided to show that particular bit of the interview in their final broadcast. It made fine TV because it was a wonderful, down-to-earth, vivid mind picture (see section below), which anybody could understand and appreciate. It brought her subject to life for a non-specialist audience in a way that any number of lengthy academic explanations would fail to do.

Secondly, by communicating in such a conversational way, she showed herself to be warm and enthusiastic about her subject and keen to share her passion for it. So the broadcasters weren't just helping themselves by showing that particular bit of her interview, they were helping her and her organization too. A classic win-win.

Remember, conversational language does *not* undermine your intelligence and authority, because true intelligence involves the ability to communicate complex subjects in the simple, comprehensible way that the media demands. But conversational language will enable you to communicate with warmth, empathy and enthusiasm *as well as* intelligence.

Tailor your language to your audience

The section above is about how best to communicate with a general audience. However, if you are communicating with a niche or specialist audience then you might be free to use more specialist terminology, so long as it's easily understood by those viewers, listeners or readers.

Imagine, for example, that you're a corporate lawyer and one of your specialist areas is international financial regulation. How far do you need to go in explaining what the Basel III regulations are all about?

- If you're doing an interview with *International Financial Law Review* magazine you wouldn't have to explain it at all. The readers will almost certainly be completely familiar with the subject already.

- For an interview with CNN (watched by an international business audience), you'll probably want to give a brief explanation to remind the viewers what Basel III is all about. Don't assume they know everything about it, but at the same time don't come across as patronizing.

- For an interview with Fox News in the US (or BBC1 in Britain, TF1 in France, or ABC in Australia etc), you'll want to spell it out properly, imagining you're talking to a group of intelligent 14-year-olds.

To illustrate this further let's look at an interview that BBC News conducted with two experts, one from Britain and one from the US, about the threat posed by a new type of software virus. On this occasion the British expert spoke more conversationally and clearly:

- What the American spokesperson said about the virus: "Basically, it's searching out all Windows NT and Windows 2000 servers that have the Microsoft web server installed that have not been patched with a widely available security patch. And basically what this worm does is installs itself on the system and then begins searching the internet for other vulnerable Windows web servers."

- What the British spokesperson said (Graham Cluley of Sophus Anti-Virus): "It is mainly businesses that are going to be affected by this. The average home user doesn't have to worry about it because they are not running web servers at their home. But if you are a business and you're running a website and you're doing it on Microsoft software then you need to download the patch from Microsoft's website to ensure that you're properly protected."

For a highly technical audience, the US spokesperson's comments might have been fine. But for a general audience (such as the BBC's) it is too technical. In contrast, Graham Cluley hit the mark.

All of these guidelines apply to print interviews just as much as to broadcast interviews. In fact you can often tell when you or your spokesperson is supplying information in a face-to-face interview to a print journalist that is too complicated or inaccessible. The journalist will instinctively stop writing and put their pen down, and will probably be thinking to themselves "When can I get out of here?"

What if you accidentally stray into jargon?

As mentioned above, it can be difficult not to use jargon if such terms are common currency within your organization or industry. So in the middle of an interview, however hard you're trying to communicate conversationally, you might occasionally drop in a piece of jargon without even realizing it.

For example, everyone in the aerospace industry knows what IATA is. But few others do (it's actually the International Air Transport Association). Now, given that people in the aerospace industry talk about IATA a lot, it makes sense for them to use the acronym when communicating with each other, rather than spelling it out all the time. And it's therefore understandable that, when doing interviews aimed at non-aerospace audiences, spokespeople will occasionally refer to IATA. The trick, here, if you find yourself straying into jargon or an acronym that your audience won't understand, is not to panic or beat yourself up about it, but just to take a moment to translate it into something the audience *will* understand.

Example

Interviewer:	How is the aerospace industry responding to this challenge?
Aerospace expert:	It's something that the industry is taking very seriously. In fact IATA is holding a conference to discuss it next week – IATA being the International Air Transport Association – and what we expect to hear is that . . .

NB Of course, if you're an aerospace expert and you're doing an interview with *Air Transport* magazine, read entirely by aerospace professionals, then there is no need to spell out IATA.

Example

Interviewer:	Why should kids stay at school after 16?
Educational expert:	Because they'll develop what educational-ists call higher-order-thinking skills, *which simply means an ability to analyse problems and complex ideas*, and such skills will help them . . .

It's important to explain jargon like this even when you're being interviewed by a print journalist, who will otherwise have to waste time translating your words into something more conversational and easy to understand for the reader – assuming they know how to do so. So be helpful, save them the bother and translate it for them, and they are more likely to come back to you for an interview next time round instead of going to one of your competitors.

Conversational language in politics

Former US president Ronald Reagan is regarded by many as one of the best communicators ever, not least because he had a knack for communicating in the most conversational English. These are some choice soundbites from his presidency:

- "You ain't seen nothin' yet!" (used many times on the campaign trail in 1984 and beyond);
- "Win one for the Gipper" (a reference to his role as George Gipp in the film *Knute Rockne, All American*);
- "There you go again" (to Jimmy Carter in a TV debate leading up to the 1979 presidential election);
- "Mr Gorbachev, tear down this wall" (overlooking the Berlin Wall);
- "A hippie is someone who looks like Tarzan, walks like Jane and smells like Cheetah."

Now, of course it's far easier to communicate in plain, conversational English when you've got a script in front of you, but Reagan also managed to communicate in this conversational style when he was being interviewed by journalists. Here are a few quotes from his interview at the White House with Merv Griffin in 1983:

- On the attempt to assassinate him: "I realize that any time I have left [Reagan looks upwards] I owe to him."

- On the economy he inherited in 1980: "When the interest rates stopped the automobile market, people couldn't afford the interest to buy cars on time and it stopped the housing industry. Either one of those industries can by themselves create a recession. And the housing industry stopped; that meant the associated industries started to dwindle – furniture, appliances, the lumbering industry and so forth. And I think that the stimulant of the economy has now seen . . . well, last month, new housing starts were at an annual rate of almost two million. The automobiles? Right now, they're having trouble keeping up with the demand."

- On unemployment: "I don't want that fellow out there waiting for a job, that's unemployed, to think we've forgotten about him. That's the end result that we're working for."

- On his route to politics: "For years and years, long before I even thought I'd be governor of California . . . I was out on the 'mashed-potato circuit'. I've always said that in Hollywood if you don't sing or dance you wind up as an after-dinner speaker. So that was what I was doing."

- On the relationship between government and business: "I thought before I came here that over the years government had formed a sort of adversary relationship with business, instead of thinking in terms of partnership and keeping the economy going, the way it should."

- On what future generations will think of his presidency: "Well I hope they won't think too harshly and, well, I hope they'll assume I did my best."

It's all beautifully conversational and natural, and if you watch the clip now (Google: "Reagan on Merv Griffin") it's easy to see why he was such a force in the 1980s. Incidentally, his body language, pace of delivery and melodious tone were simply world class.

Politicians don't, by any means, always set a perfect example when it comes to media-interview techniques (see the section on "Avoiding the question" in Chapter 7), but spokespeople and their advisers can learn a lot from the ability of many politicians to speak in plain, conversational English. US presidents (Bill Clinton also springs to mind) are particularly good at this, but many other leaders have mastered it too because, frankly, that's how they get elected. And those that find it difficult to speak conversationally, such as the former British prime minister Gordon Brown, sometimes also find it difficult to make a connection with the voters.

A more recent example of an interviewee with a great tone of voice comes from 14 April 2014. John Humphrys of the BBC Radio 4 *Today Programme* interviewed Ruth Davison, director of policy for the National Housing Federation, on the government's proposal to give housing association tenants the right to buy the homes they live in. Davison opposed the government's plans, and she explained why in clear, conversational English. This is how the interview went:

Humphrys:	Why don't you approve?
Davison:	Look, we costed this policy. We made a very conservative estimate of £5.8 billion. That's what we thought it might cost.
Humphrys:	How can it cost to sell something?
Davison:	Oh, because it needs to be funded by the taxpayer. Housing associations are independent organizations and charities. You can no more force housing associations to sell their assets at less than they are worth than you could force Tesco's to sell their assets [Humphrys tries to interrupt], or even cancer research, so housing associations would have to be fully recompensed for any sale . . .
Humphrys:	Any sale that produces less than the value of the house.
Davison:	Indeed, so there will be a cost to the taxpayer. We estimated – a conservative estimate – £5.8 billion. I see the briefing in the papers this morning is saying almost £20 billion. And what I would say is half way through a programme of austerity and in the grips of

a housing crisis if you had £20 billion of taxpayer's money would you just give it away as a gift to some of the most securely housed people in the country on some of the lowest rents?

[The interview then goes briefly onto the subject of people aspiring to own their own homes before Davison returns to what she considers to be the housing priority.]

Davison:	But listen, there are nine million private renters in this country who would also like to own their own home, who are paying much, much higher rents than the social and affordable rents that people in housing associations properties are paying. And three million adult children are living at home who in some instances can't even afford that rent. We have an affordability crisis. We have a housing crisis. If, thankfully, we now have some proper decent money to spend on housing, let's not just give it away to really well-housed people on low rents.
Humphrys:	What would you do with it then?
Davison:	If those figures in this morning's papers are right, you could build one million shared-ownership properties.
Humphrys:	And what if your figures are right? £5.8 billion.
Davison:	Well you could build a third of that. You could build 300,000 shared-ownership properties and give 300,000 people a foot on the housing ladder. Or, God forbid, we could build some social housing. But there are ways that we could spend this money that would not be a costly distraction because the government would need to legislate to force housing associations to dispose of their assets . . .
Humphrys:	It could be immensely politically popular!
Davison:	It could be, but it could also be immensely popular politically if we built a million shared-ownership homes that would be available for everybody, and give everybody a chance to get a foot on the housing ladder.
Humphrys:	Ruth Davison, thank you very much.

By keeping things simple, speaking in conversational English and sticking to terminology that the audience of the *Today Programme* would understand, Davison's tone was warm and enthusiastic as well as intelligent and sincere. As a result she came across as entirely natural and believable.

2 Using mind pictures

The second way to convey warmth, enthusiasm and empathy is through mind pictures. In Chapter 3, we discussed the power of mind pictures to support key messages and make them complete. But they are doubly important because they also have the power to give the interviewee warmth, empathy and enthusiasm. In fact, they can do that for interviewees who would otherwise come across as bland, boring and cold. They really are that powerful.

Imagine if the educational expert described above had used a mind picture during her interview. She'd instantly have transformed her tone of voice from cool and report-like to warm and friendly. So having finished talking about the importance of continuing at school after the age of 16, she might have added: "I remember a student we had at this college 10 years ago. He was 16, and had achieved some good exam results, but was desperate to leave school and start earning money. So his parents and I spoke to him and persuaded him to stay on. He did so, and then went on to university. Well, I saw him again just last week, and I have to say I hardly recognized him in his very smart suit. He's now an accountant at one of the big firms, and he told me how grateful he was that we persuaded him to stay on at school all those years ago. In fact he said it transformed his life, which was lovely to hear."

As we saw in Chapter 3, the mind picture you create might not necessarily be a nice, happy picture. It might be an unpleasant one, which is fine so long as it serves your message. And these unpleasant mind pictures still enable you to come across as warm and empathetic. So, for example, the educational expert might say:

"I've known so many students who have left school at 16 and then regretted it. In fact, one young woman particularly sticks in my memory. She could have stayed on at our college beyond 16, but chose to leave because that's what some of her friends were doing. She's now in her late 20s, and she told me recently that she bitterly regrets not carrying on with her education and pursuing her dream of becoming an engineer. She's certainly got the intelligence for it, but now she feels it's too late."

Colour, personality and emotion

As we discussed in Chapter 3, the best mind pictures have personal, emotional content, showing the audience that the interviewee really cares about their message.

However, with the best will in the world, some subjects – high finance, for example, or regulatory initiatives – are really pretty dry and therefore difficult to support with pictures. So as well as using analogies and metaphors to develop mind pictures on such subjects, you can bring in colour and personality by:

Gentle self-mockery:

- "This is the sort of new initiative that gets boring lawyers like me really excited . . ."
- "Okay, I wouldn't discuss it with someone on a hot date, but it really is going to have a big effect . . ."

Expressive language:

- "This is the holy grail of financial regulation."
- "The financial services industry can no longer keep its head stuck in the sand about this one."
- "We've been waiting two long years for this decision, and thank God the moment has finally arrived."

In the previous chapter, I used UK personal finance expert Martin Lewis as an example of someone with a naturally enthusiastic voice. But he doesn't just rely on vocal modulation to convey enthusiasm. He also uses graphic language. For instance, in November 2013 he was interviewed on ITV's *This Morning* show (watched by a broad general audience in the UK) about how to improve your credit rating score, which is hardly the most fascinating subject in the world. But a little way into the interview, Lewis said: "What we're trying to do is to make you more attractive, and it's a bit like going 'on the pull'. Now when you go on the pull there's things you can do to make yourself more attractive to many people . . ." By comparing personal finance to dating, Lewis made the whole subject a whole lot more interesting. He brought it to life.

No viewer or listener is going to be any more enthused by your subject than you yourself are, or than you show yourself to be. So, as Sue Milne wrote in *Management Magazine* (February 2008): "Why not take a wee risk now and then? Add a bit of colour, celebrate the English language in all its rich and varied glory, soar above the humdrum, meaningless waffle of super-safe business speak."

All elements of W.I.S.E. working together

The best interviewees are able to convey, in equal measure, warmth, intelligence, sincerity, enthusiasm and empathy. If they do so, they have the perfect tone of voice for any kind of media interview.

In their book *Compelling People: The hidden qualities that make us influential* (2014), John Neffinger and Matthew Kohut describe the two key attributes that successful people have: strength and warmth. Finding the balance between the two can be difficult to achieve, but it's the key to success. It is, say Neffinger and Kohut, "where the people we call 'charismatic' hang out."

In media interviews, strength is conveyed by an intelligent and sincere tone of voice (as well as strong body language and a strong message). We *respect* such spokespeople. Meanwhile, enthusiasm and empathy add to a spokesperson's warmth. We *like* such spokespeople.

So next time you or your spokesperson is preparing to do an interview, think about how you can project both strength and warmth – how you can make yourself respected and liked. If you're successful, the chances are that your interview will go really well.

Curtailing your curtness

There is a fine line between coming across as a straight-talker who says it like it is (usually a good thing) and being curt and blunt (often a bad thing).

In Chapter 4 we spoke about the need to keep your cool in interviews, including the need to keep your temper and anger under control. But actually, interviewees who come across as rude or curt often do so without realizing it. Their only intention, typically, is to get straight to the point and waste as few words as necessary.

As a rule of thumb, if the interviewee's answers are, on average, shorter than the journalist's questions, that interviewee is in danger of conveying curtness. Imagine, for example, that you represent a manufacturer and you or your spokesperson is being interviewed by a regional radio station about your sponsorship of the town's football team. Then towards the end of the interview the reporter throws in a few questions about your plans for expanding the factory. The interview could go like this:

Reporter: Everyone in this town is keen to know when your factory is going to expand further and take on more staff. Is there anything you can tell us about that?

Spokesperson: We have no plans for expansion at the moment.

Reporter: Can I at least take it that you aren't planning any redundancies?

Spokesperson: We aren't planning any redundancies.

Reporter: I understand you're planning a partnership with local schools in this area, to give work placements to teenagers. When can we expect to hear more about that?

Spokesperson: Maybe later this year. Our plans are at an early stage.

Now, in this case, the spokesperson may have good reason for wanting to keep his cards close to his chest about those particular subjects. Perhaps going any further on any of them will get him and his organization into trouble. But he can come across as a lot less curt, and a lot warmer and more likeable, simply by fleshing out his answers while giving nothing further away. For example:

Reporter: Everyone in this town is keen to know when your factory is going to expand further and take on more staff. Is there anything you can tell us about that?

Spokesperson: Yes, I know everyone wants to hear our plans, and of course they are entitled to know as soon as we have anything concrete to tell them. I have to say, however, that we have no plans for expansion at the moment. The factory currently employs 320 staff, including contractors, and that's the way it's going to stay for now. But, as I say, we are committed to communicating everything to the local community, so we'll let people know as soon as things change.

Reporter: Can I at least take it that you aren't planning any redundancies?

Spokesperson: That's another important point for the local community, and it's always something we're asked about. Of course, we can't predict everything that's going to happen in the coming months and years, but I can assure you that we aren't planning any redundancies at the moment.

Reporter: I understand you're planning a partnership with local schools in this area, to give work placements to teenagers. When can we expect to hear more about that?

Spokesperson: A partnership with local schools is something our company is looking at, and we always want to give teenagers a taste of working life. Currently our plans are at a very early stage, and we're giving plenty of thought to which route to take. We think we'll be able to tell you more later this year when we've looked at things in a bit more detail.

In each of these answers, the spokesperson is giving away no more concrete information than in the first set of much shorter, curter answers. But by fleshing the answers out a bit, and showing he understands the way local people feel about important matters to them, and even shares some of those feelings, he comes across as a lot warmer and more empathetic.

Finding the full stop

Whereas some people need to curtail their curtness, others need to curtail their natural verbosity. Such people meander on and on, making the interview sound more like a monologue or an impenetrable stream of consciousness. Often, the only way the journalist can make it interactive (ie an interview) is simply to butt in.

Again, people who are verbose don't usually do so intentionally. They just have trouble finding that elusive full stop – the natural conclusion to their thoughts. Period.

So what can help them?

1 **The message sandwich** (see Chapter 3). If you structure your answer as a message sandwich, you will naturally reach a conclusion, preventing any flabby verbosity.

2 **Bridging** (see Chapter 7). Spend the minimum amount of time answering a question that is irrelevant to your key messages before "bridging" to something you consider more important.

3 **Looking at the journalist's eyes.** It's usually quite obvious if a journalist is losing interest. Their eyes visibly glaze over. If that happens, reach your conclusion as quickly as possible.

4 **Practising.** If you know what you want to say and how you're going to say it you'll be much less likely to waffle.

5 **Just stop talking.** It's as simple as that.

Humour

There is a place for humour in media interviews – in certain situations. If, for example, the person being interviewed makes their living as a stand-up comedian, then it would look fairly odd if they didn't try to be funny in media interviews.

But most spokespeople are simply representing their entirely non-comic organization. And attempts at humour are, in many circumstances, simply distracting, inappropriate or just plain embarrassing. Or at least they are if they go beyond a gentle quip or amusing anecdote.

For example, early in 2013, European supermarkets faced a major crisis when it was revealed by the Irish Food Standards Agency that many of the beef products these supermarkets sold contained horsemeat. This caused understandable consumer disgust and alarm throughout the continent. To counter this, Malcolm Walker, the CEO of British supermarket chain Iceland, invited the BBC into one of his stores to talk about the scandal. This was part of the exchange:

Reporter:　How can you sell a product if you don't really know what's in it?

Walker:　I know exactly what's in our products. I've just told you! It says on that burger that we've just looked at 78 per cent beef. B.E.E.F. Beef. That's what's in our burgers.

Reporter:　I know, but the Irish say that there is point one per cent of H.O.R.S.E. Horse.

Walker:　Well, that's the Irish isn't it.

Walker delivered these lines with a smile and twinkly eye, and the last line was accompanied by a humorous little shrug and playful grin. Humour may serve him well in many circumstances, but was this the time and place for such joshing, when consumers were genuinely horrified by the issue of horsemeat – a horror that he dismissed with an apparently racist remark? Probably not. Walker might have done better to play it straight, even if he did think that the crisis was all a bit of "a storm in a tea cup".

A handful of my interviewees have, over the years, found it difficult to resist the temptation to try and be funny during media interviews, and they nearly always fall flat. Of course, it's easy to come up with exceptions to the keep-it-straight rule. Boris Johnson, mayor of

London, has built much of his enormous public profile on humour, complete with what looks like a comedy blond wig. And he has been hugely successful. But even he knows when to stop, such as when there were riots throughout London during August 2011.

Frankly, Boris is a one-off. And it's best not to try to copy him.

Summary

1 Try to project W.I.S.E. – warmth, intelligence, sincerity and enthusiasm/empathy.

2 To ensure you project sincerity, be certain that you have examples and evidence to back up your key messages.

3 To project warmth, enthusiasm and empathy, keep your delivery as conversational as possible by cutting out jargon and corporate-speak . . .

4 . . . and remember the vital importance of mind pictures.

5 For media interviews aimed at a general, non-specialist audience, imagine you're talking to a group of intelligent 14-year-olds.

6 If you accidentally stray into jargon, just calmly spell out what you mean.

7 If your natural tendency is to be blunt, curtail it by fleshing out your answer meaningfully.

8 If your natural tendency is to waffle, find the full stop by structuring your answer as a message sandwich.

9 If in doubt, leave the humour out.

Exercises

1 Think about your natural communications style. Which elements of W.I.S.E. (warm, intelligent, sincere and enthusiastic/empathetic) do you most need to work on?

2 Have you got the examples and evidence you need to support your key messages, which will ensure you communicate sincerely?

3 Think of some examples of jargon or corporate-speak in your industry. How might you translate them into something more conversational and everyday for a general audience?

4 What kind of mind pictures could you paint in order to communicate in a warm, enthusiastic and empathetic way?

5 Do you tend to be too blunt? If so, how might you flesh out your answers to make you sound warmer and less defensive?

6 Do you tend to be too verbose? If so, practise structuring your answers as message sandwiches to help you find the full stop.

Keeping control of the interview

07

In this chapter we consider the main techniques for ensuring that your message becomes the focal point of the interview. After all, there is no point in having two or three beautifully prepared messages, with accompanying examples and evidence, if you never get to use them.

Keeping control of the interview does not mean that the journalist loses control. It is not a winner-takes-all battle. The ideal is that the journalist *and* interviewee both get what they're looking for. A win-win.

ABC: the bridging technique

Bridging is a technique of fundamental importance to media interviews, and is one that media trainers have been teaching for years. It means that you can always get to your key messages and that you or your spokesperson will never have the excuse of going back to the office after an interview and saying to your colleagues: "I'm afraid I didn't say my key messages because the right questions didn't come up." Once you've perfected bridging, you'll *always* be able to get to your messages, regardless of the questions.

Bridging involves three simple stages:

Stage 1: Answer/Address the question.

Stage 2: Bridge.

Stage 3: Communicate your message.

Stage 1: Answer/address the question

When a journalist asks a question the interviewee has two main options:

1 Answer the question.

2 Address the question.

Obviously a journalist wants you to answer the question, and that should always be your default choice. However, there are some questions that you cannot or should not answer, because it would get you or your organization into trouble. For example, you shouldn't answer a question if:

- You haven't been briefed on that particular subject;
- It would be unwise to speculate about something;
- There are security considerations;
- There are data-privacy considerations;
- The information the journalist is asking for is confidential;
- Your organization has a policy not to reveal that particular information.

When you *address* the question you simply tell the journalist *why you cannot answer it*. And journalists accept that, though they might not always like it, because they understand that not every piece of information they ask for can be supplied. But they do expect to be told the reason, and it has to be better than "I cannot comment on that" (see section on "No comment" below).

Stages 2 and 3: Bridge and communicate

When you have answered or addressed the question, you can then go straight into a bridging expression, such as:

- The important point is . . .
- I'd also like to add . . .
- My key message is this . . .
- What our customers care about is . . .
- What's important to remember . . .

- And that's why we always say . . .
- To put this in context . . .
- But our focus is on . . .
- But while that's true, we mustn't forget . . .
- However . . .
- But . . .

All these expressions allow you to bridge, or pivot, the conversation away from a question that is negative, or simply irrelevant to your messages. You are then free to communicate your key message.

You should aim to spend *the minimum amount of time, to satisfy the journalist,* answering or addressing a question that is irrelevant to your key messages. After all, you don't want to spend two minutes of a three-minute interview answering a question that has nothing to do with your key messages. That minimum amount of time may take you 10 or 20 seconds. On the other hand it might take you only two or three seconds.

A good example of bridging was demonstrated by a British Medical Association (BMA) spokesperson, Dr Sam Everington, when he was interviewed live on BBC TV about the effects of passive smoking. The interview was prefaced by a clip of a smoker declaring his right to smoke, on the grounds that he lives in a free country. The presenter then asked Everington whether he agreed that the smoker had a right to smoke. His answer was a perfect demonstration of bridging: "I would defend his right to smoke. But I would equally expect him to defend the right of a non-smoker not to have smoke imposed on them. And that's the key issue. It's not about stopping him from smoking. It's giving people – sometimes the most vulnerable and poorer members of our society – the right not to have people smoke in their workplaces or in public places."

We can break that answer down into the three stages of bridging:

1 **Answer:** "I would defend his right to smoke."

2 **Bridge:** "But I would equally expect him to defend the right of a non-smoker not to have smoke imposed on them. And that's the key issue."

3 **Communicate the message:** "It's not about stopping him from smoking. It's giving people – sometimes the most vulnerable

and poorer members of our society – the right not to have people smoke in their workplaces or in public places."

That was a smooth, seamless bridge, with Stage 1 taking no more than two seconds. But sometimes you have to resort to a rather more clunky bridge in order to communicate your key message, and that's better than no bridge at all. Imagine you're a spokesperson for a pharmaceuticals company and you're doing an interview about a new treatment for asthma. Your key message might be "This drug needs to be taken just once a week" (in contrast to most asthma drugs that need to be taken at least once a day). But the journalist's question is: "How effective is this new drug in treating asthma?"

You might answer: "It's very successful. In clinical trials, the drug improved the condition of children even with severe asthma. However, the real benefit is that it only needs to be taken once a week . . ." The bridging expression "However, the real benefit is . . ." switches the conversation onto the interviewee's key message, even though it isn't directly related to the question.

If you or your spokesperson are getting towards the end of the interview and are yet to communicate one of your key messages, you might have to resort to the clunkiest of all bridges, such as:

- There's something else I'd like to add before we finish . . .
- Another topic I haven't yet mentioned is . . .
- The final message I have is . . .

It's easier to come up with one of these clunky bridges during print interviews, as opposed to broadcast interviews, as a print journalist will often ask at the end of an interview if there's anything else you or your spokesperson would like to add. That's an invitation for you to communicate your final message, or re-emphasize messages you've already given.

The helicopter technique

One of the best ways to answer a negative question is to broaden the issue out so that it doesn't just focus upon you or your organization.

In effect, you are inviting the journalist to journey upwards, and look at the bigger picture, from the vantage point of a helicopter.

For example, imagine you're a spokesperson for an oil company, and you're questioned about the pollution your operations cause. You might use the helicopter technique by saying: "The oil industry *as a whole* faces these issues, and we know we need to do better. That's why we're working together to solve them . . ."

Or suppose you represent a university, and you're asked by a local newspaper reporter about an increasing number of drop-outs among first-year students. You might reply: "Yes, it's something we're concerned about, and it's an issue than *many universities* are having to confront . . ."

The caving technique

The opposite of the helicopter technique is what I call the "caving technique". This is where you take the journalist on a journey downwards, *within your organization*, which can be useful if you are asked something negative about the organization as a whole.

For instance, suppose you work for the French office of an international courier company. In years gone by your company described itself as "The best courier company in the world", but more recently the company has suffered badly in comparison to new market entrants. A journalist may ask you "Are you still 'The best courier company in the world'?" Using the caving technique you can dig down into your own department (the French office) and say: "Here in France our customers definitely think so, yes. And let me explain why . . ."

Avoiding the question – rarely a good idea

There is all the difference in the world between *addressing* the question and *avoiding* it. Avoiding the question (dodging, ducking or ignoring it) is something that misguided politicians do far too often, and it's one of the things that gives them a bad name. It is also profoundly irritating for the journalist and the watching and listening public.

Typically, politicians avoid the question by answering one that they wish had been asked instead. For example:

Journalist:	You said your government would cut unemployment. Actually, it's gone up. Why is that?
Politician:	Under this government the economy has improved dramatically, with companies investing more than ever before . . .

Journalist:	Have you ever taken illegal drugs?
Politician:	I've always said that drugs are tremendously harmful to society, and we must do all we can to stop their use . . .

In a famous BBC TV interview in 1997, the then British Home Secretary, Michael Howard, avoided the same question from the presenter, Jeremy Paxman, an incredible 14 times in a row. Nearly 20 years later, Howard is still trying to live that one down. (Google "Paxman v Howard 1997" to see the whole exchange.)

You would have thought that politicians might have learned from Howard's experience, but apparently not. Take Chloe Smith, a junior minister in the British government between 2010 and 2013. In 2012 she was interviewed by Paxman about the government's decision to abandon its plans to raise tax on fuel. Watching it now (Google: "Paxman v Chloe Smith") is like witnessing a 12-minute car crash, and it gets particularly painful at the three-minute mark, where Smith nearly grinds to a halt and has to lunge for a glass of water. But it all started to go wrong with her avoidance, six times, of the very first question:

Paxman:	When were you told of this change of plan?
Smith:	Well as a minister in the Treasury, and indeed dealing with fuel matters, this has been under consideration for some time . . .
Paxman:	When was the decision taken?
Smith:	As I say, it's been under consideration for some time, the chancellor and the prime minister . . .
Paxman:	Yes of course, so when were you told?
Smith:	I've been involved in this for some time, and . . .

Paxman:	But you didn't take the decision, obviously, so when were you told?
Smith:	We had a collective discussion in due course and although I can't give you the full gory details . . .
Paxman:	Did it happen today?
Smith:	I can't sit here and tell you the ins and the outs . . .
Paxman:	You can't remember?
Smith:	No, it's not appropriate for me to tell you the ins and the outs . . .
Paxman:	Why isn't it appropriate?

From this low starting point, the interview continued to go downhill. Why Smith felt she had to avoid that first question instead of just answering it is quite beyond me. If she had just said: "I was told of the final decision this morning", or "We took the decision in a meeting I took part in this afternoon", the interview as a whole would have been better from her point of view. And would such an admission really have been so damaging to her and the government?

The distinguished British columnist Matthew Parris has made an admirable attempt to defend politicians who avoid questions. Writing in *The Times* on 10 May 2014, he encapsulated the conundrum politicians face when being interviewed, concluding that those who "hedge, bluster, flannel and obfuscate" (ie avoid questions) are, paradoxically, the honest ones, on the grounds that they are simply trying to avoid saying something that isn't true while still remaining faithful to their political party.

Parris might be right that such politicians are honest. And, of course, they shouldn't lie. But avoiding pertinent questions makes the interviewee appear insincere, arrogant, untrustworthy and slippery. So I disagree with Parris on this one.

Some politicians seem to think that *every* question is a banana skin. It's rumoured that the former British prime minister Gordon Brown even had to ask his advisers how to respond to a question about his favourite type of biscuit, so keen was he to see the hidden danger in every question. No doubt there are *a few* questions where answering truthfully can damage the interviewee even more than ducking them.

But not many, and being asked for your favourite biscuit certainly isn't one of them. In any case, there is *always* a way that you can find to address the question rather than ignore it.

For example, Gordon Brown's successor, David Cameron, has repeatedly refused to answer questions about whether he has ever taken illegal drugs. But he doesn't *avoid* the question. Instead, he *addresses* it by saying that he feels he's entitled to keep his life before he entered politics private. Okay, it's a pretty flimsy reason for not answering the question, and it's one that might lead people to conclude that Cameron did indeed take drugs, perhaps while at university. But it's better to give a flimsy reason than to give no reason at all.

In fact, Cameron's former number two as deputy prime minister, Nick Clegg, might have been well advised to follow the prime minister's example when faced with an intensely personal question of his own shortly after becoming leader of the Liberal Democrats. During an interview with *GQ Magazine*, the journalist Piers Morgan asked Clegg how many women he'd slept with during his life. Incredibly, Clegg chose to answer. "No more than 30," he declared, before then giving an appraisal of his skills in the bedroom.

We can give Clegg full marks for honesty, but surely this is a question that it would be better for an aspiring statesman to address rather than answer ("I hope you will forgive me for not answering such a personal question, but what I can say is . . ."). A media interview is not like being in a court of law. Just because the journalist asks you a question, you don't *have* to answer it. But make sure you address it. (In fact some journalists have an instinct to ask the most outlandish questions possible, hoping you will answer but not really expecting you to. They are amazed when you do.)

If you are ever tempted to avoid the question altogether, ask yourself this: are you absolutely sure that portraying yourself to be untrustworthy and slippery (the inevitable consequence of avoidance) is less damaging to your reputation than answering the question?

While politicians are infamous avoiders, a handful of businesspeople are just as bad. A famous example dates from 2013 when Stephen Bates, then the European managing director of the Canadian company Research In Motion (now known as BlackBerry Ltd), chose, needlessly, to avoid just about every question from a business reporter during a live TV interview. The main question, an entirely reasonable one, was why his company had struggled in recent years, losing market share to rivals like Apple and Samsung. This was the main part of the exchange:

Reporter: You've got a lot of catching up to do though, haven't you? Because your global share of the smartphone market has fallen from a peak of around 20 per cent back in 2009 to 6 per cent today.

Bates: Actually we've got around 79 million customers today. There's a loyal bunch of BlackBerry users out there, so we're really excited today to bring them something really different – something that bridges the world of the consumer and the business user through something we're calling BlackBerry Balance.

Reporter: You must admit though that it's been a tough few years for you. You've seen your market share fall nearly 90 per cent from its peak in 2008. What went wrong?

Bates: So I'm always excited to be part of this industry. I'm proud to be part of this industry. This is a really exciting industry to be in. We're at the verge of this major change towards mobile computing and we think BlackBerry 10 is going to power us through the next 10 years. We're really excited.

Reporter: What went wrong?

Bates: Fundamentally this is a great market and I think we've been brave, we've tried lots of things. We were at the start of the smartphone business. We're really at the cusp of the change of this market now. And the uniqueness around BlackBerry 10 . . . we've taken the decision to build our own operating system and that gives us the ability to control this brand-new user experience we'll be talking about this afternoon.

Reporter: But you still haven't told me what went wrong.

Bates: This is a phenomenal market. We're brave. We're out there. We're pushing it. We've transitioned and are supporting a business in the consumer world and in the business world and for us what's important is ensuring that we deliver a great unique experience to those 79 million customers out there and all the other BlackBerry users that we think we'll get.

Reporter: Okay Stephen. We might never know what went wrong, but anyway thanks very much for your time.

At that point the camera panned to the two main studio presenters, one of whom joked to the other: "So what was it that went wrong?". (To see the whole interview, Google "Stephen Bates, RIM BBC interview".)

Of all the interviews I've seen in recent years, this was one of the worst from the point of view of the company being interviewed, and as a result it makes great TV. Bates' avoidance of just about every question is very unwise, leaving the audience unable to concentrate on anything else. And yet how different it would have been, and how much better, if he'd just answered the question before bridging to his key message:

Reporter: You've got a lot of catching up to do though, haven't you? Because your global share of the smartphone market has fallen from a peak of around 20 per cent back in 2009 to 6 per cent today.

What Bates
could have said: Of course we're disappointed that our market share hasn't been as good recently as before. Perhaps we took things for granted, and let our competitors get ahead of us. But even so, there's a loyal bunch of 79 million Blackberry users out there, so we're really excited today to bring them something that bridges the world of the consumer and the business user through something we're calling Blackberry Balance . . ."

If he'd taken that open approach the rest of the interview (all 95 per cent of it) might well have focused on what RIM was doing to recover its position in the market. He might even have got to explain what Blackberry Balance was all about. Instead, and quite rightly, the journalist repeatedly asked the same negative question.

To be fair to Bates, he was possibly badly media trained, and obviously he hadn't read this book, so it wasn't all his own fault. Nevertheless, it doesn't take a public-relations genius to work out that avoiding every question will, in itself, become the story of the interview.

"No comment"

Saying "No comment" or "I cannot comment" is the most extreme way of avoiding a question. Some of my trainees over the years have used one or both of these phrases in their opening practice interviews when asked about sensitive issues facing their organization. When I ask them why, after the interview, they typically say that the information being asked for is none of the media's business. Well, fine. Perhaps it isn't any of their business. But that won't stop the journalist asking the question, and you can be sure that if you say "No comment" the audience will always assume the worst.

For instance, suppose your company runs 10 factories throughout the country, and is at the very earliest stages of deciding whether to close one of them and relocate the workforce. A radio reporter accosts you at the factory gates, and asks you about your plans:

Reporter:	Does your company plan to close this factory, with the loss of 5,000 jobs?
Spokesperson:	No comment.

Audience assumption: The factory is about to close and 5,000 people are going to lose their jobs.

However, if you answer the question honestly and openly, the audience won't jump to the most negative conclusion:

Reporter:	Does your company plan to close this factory, with the loss of 5,000 jobs?
Spokesperson:	At the moment we're in the earliest stages of deciding what to do with our 10 factories throughout the country, and while we can never guarantee that any factory will stay open for ever, we have no immediate plans to close any of our factories.

> We are looking at the options, however, and we'll keep our workforce throughout the country fully informed.

Audience assumption: *Those 5,000 jobs seem to be safe for now.*

In summary, only say "No comment" if you're happy for the audience to assume the worst.

Repetition of key messages

In any interview of any length, you should aim to repeat your messages as often as necessary to make them stand out and unmissable. In Figure 7.1 you'll see the timeline of a five-minute interview. Across the middle are all the journalist's question – good ones, easy ones, searching ones and ignorant ones. And at the bottom are your messages. Your job in any interview is to bridge to your messages as early as possible, and repeat them as often as necessary, perhaps with a slightly different wording each time, to make them stand out.

Within reason, repetition of your key messages is a very good idea. I've been lucky enough to travel to the Falkland Islands on two occasions to media train politicians and other leading citizens, focusing on the right of the islanders to remain British if they so choose. There were interviews I conducted there during which interviewees

FIGURE 7.1   Bridge as often as necessary

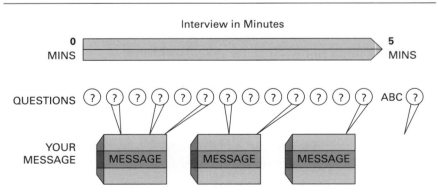

SOURCE copyright Robert Taylor Communications

would repeat the same key message about the importance of self-determination four or five times in a short interview. It did not look or sound excessive. It was just one of the ways in which they made their message stand out and unmissable.

A few years ago, I arranged for Peter Mandelson, one of the architects of the success of Britain's Labour Party during the 1990s, to deliver a presentation to one of my clients about communications and messaging. I remember to this day his key piece of advice: "It is only when you are sick to death of hearing yourself repeat the same message over and over again that your audience is just beginning to get it."

Repeat your message as often as necessary, across one interview or several interviews, until your audience *gets it*. At the end of your interview it should be completely obvious to your audience what your key message is, giving you the best chance that they will remember and act on it. It's unlikely that they will do so if you simply mumble it once halfway through.

Notwithstanding that, it is possible to *over*-repeat a message by trying to shoehorn it into every answer. And that can make you look extremely foolish. In 2011, Britain's Labour Party leader, Ed Miliband, did a recorded interview for the BBC about a day of public-sector strikes, and gave exactly the same answer five times in a row. So keen was he to make sure that his prepared soundbite was the only piece of the interview that the journalist could possibly use in the final broadcast that he abandoned any attempt to address the questions put to him. The journalist was so peeved that he posted the whole thing on YouTube. (Google "Ed Miliband repeats answer 2011").

Like Stephen Bates, I'm sure that Miliband was merely following the advice he'd been given. In fact, for years, some media and PR strategists have told their clients that a recorded interview is an opportunity to deliver one key message really well, and that you should carry on repeating that message whatever the question. But Miliband took that advice to an extreme.

By all means try to communicate your message as well as possible. By all means try to repeat it, within reason. But don't ever give the impression of being slavishly devoted to it, and desperate to exert total authority over the journalist's editorial judgement. Simply, if you adhere to your message so doggedly that you fail to answer questions on other topics, the audience notices and in the worst case will simply laugh at you.

Anyone preparing for a recorded interview should treat it exactly as they would a live interview. Trust yourself to bridge back to your message or messages just as you would in a live interview, but always answer or address the question first. Then, if you've done your job, and your message is compelling enough, the editor will broadcast that message and nothing else.

How to get off to a good start in a live broadcast interview

As we discussed in Chapter 4, live broadcast interviews can be nerve-racking, which is why it's so important to ease the tension by getting off to a good start. But how do you give yourself the best chance to do so?

Many media trainers around the world advise their clients to ask the reporter or presenter, just before the start of the interview (off air, obviously), what the first question will be. Just having a few seconds' notice of that first question helps the interviewee enormously, allowing them a bit of thinking time to consider their first answer and any bridge that might be necessary to get straight into their first key message.

However, the wording "What's your first question?" has some disadvantages:

1 It can irritate the presenter or reporter. Sometimes, the presenter or reporter won't know *exactly* what their first question will be literally until they start speaking, and it can be annoying to have to commit to a particular form of words before the interview starts.

2 It's a dead give-away that you've been media trained. Now, journalists should not object to the fact that you've been media trained (not if you've been trained well, anyway – see Chapter 1), but it's surely better for them simply to be impressed by your interview style and your ability to help

them create a great story for their viewers and listeners than to suspect before the interview even starts that you've just been on a training course. (Some journalists might even think to themselves: "Right sunshine, I'll show you!")

So, rather than asking "What's your first question?", ask the reporter or presenter: "How are you thinking of starting the interview?" This elicits the same information, but is softer and less confrontational.

Of course, it may not be possible to ask the reporter or presenter anything at all before the interview starts. The presenter might, for example, finish a live item and then go straight into yours. But if you do have a few seconds to ask something before the interview starts, put that time to good use. And always be aware that the journalist's first question just might be linked to the subject matter of the previous item, even if that has nothing to do with the main subject of your interview.

Handling unfair questions

Unfair questions are those where a direct answer will always get the interviewee into trouble. Heads I win, tails you lose.

Of course journalists can pretty well ask any question they like, and there's not much you can do to stop them. What's more, they might ask unfair questions for two good journalistic reasons:

1 To catch you out and make a headline. James Reston, former executive editor of the *New York Times*, said: "Great journalists know how to persuade people to say things they did not intend to say."

2 To simplify things. Journalists are there to "explain, simplify, clarify", wrote Alfred Harmsworth, founder of the *Daily Mail*.

So it's inevitable that you or your spokesperson will have to contend with unfair questions at some point, and there's no use complaining. Instead, focus on how best to answer such questions.

Here's how to deal with:

- The negative summary: "So what you're saying is that your competitor's products are dangerous. Is that it?"
  - "What I'm saying is that consumers need to look at the evidence . . ."

- The impossible guarantee: "Can you guarantee you'll never close that factory?"
  - "What I *can* guarantee is that we will always strive to keep open . . ."

- The hypothetical: "If your annual results are worse than you expect, what then?"
  - "We can't see into the future, but what I can say . . ."

- Yes or no: "Do you agree with flexible working – yes or no?"
  - "Flexible working can be useful, but is not always appropriate . . ."

- Damned either way: "Are you still treating your staff with contempt?"
  - "We've always treated our staff with respect . . ."

- Negative opinions: "Your former employee Jo Bloggs says you neglect health and safety. Why?"
  - "We see the health and safety of our employees as our top priority, which is why . . ."

- The unnecessary choice: "What do you put first, your customers or your profits?"
  - "Obviously both are important, which is why . . ."

Two key techniques for answering unfair questions

"What I can say is . . ."

Journalists are fond of presenting you with questions that invite one of only two answers (yes or no, right or wrong, black or white). For example: "Who's better at this, men or women?"

When asked such a question the temptation is to leap into one of the two boxes the journalist has presented. That might be fine on some occasions, but on others you might find yourself in a snake pit. And, in any case, the truth is often more nuanced than the journalist might be implying. So take a breath and then say "What I can say is . . ." before giving your considered response: "What I can say is that men and women have different strengths in this field . . ."

"What I can say is . . ." gives you a platform for finding the middle way between what might be two simplistic and dangerous options that the journalist is offering.

Try not to repeat a negative

Journalists are fond of making statements, and then inviting the interviewee to agree or disagree: "Your human rights record is appalling, isn't it?"

When asked such a question, the natural human instinct is simply to deny it: "No, our human rights record is not appalling." But making such a statement opens up the possibility that a print journalist could use that quote in the article – or even put it in the headline. Or a TV producer might use that soundbite from your interview, and no other. Far better, then, to respond with your own words: "Our human rights record is actually very good . . ."

Of all the techniques in this book, this is possibly the most difficult to master, because the instinct to deny an unfair accusation is so strong. Even Richard Nixon, a former US president, once said live in a press conference: "People have got to know whether or not their president is a crook. Well, I am not a crook" – thereby guaranteeing that the quote would be for ever associated with him. "I'm an honest man" might have been a better choice, even if subsequent events would disprove it.

The honest truth

Talking of Richard Nixon, of all the sins that you might be tempted to commit in a media interview, lying is by far the greatest. (Boring the audience is the second greatest.) As in life generally, honesty is your best weapon.

That doesn't mean that you need to *volunteer* something your organization has done wrong – unless you know for sure the journalist is going to ask you about it anyway – just as in a job interview you wouldn't volunteer all the mistakes you've made in your career. But you should be ready to deal with any questions about those mistakes, before moving on to something more positive.

It can be uncomfortable to answer questions, honestly, about mistakes, but in the long run you'll be far better served by doing so.

If you are ever tempted to lie to the media, just remember the experience of British politician Chris Huhne, a senior government minister between 2010 and 2012. In May 2011, Huhne's estranged wife claimed that he had "pressurized people to take his driving licence penalty points" on his behalf several years before. Huhne repeatedly denied this in interview after interview, and tried every means at his disposal to prevent the matter from coming to court.

One of his lines (and lies) was: "These allegations are simply incorrect. They've been made before and they've been shown to be untrue and I very much welcome the referral to the police as it will draw a line under the matter." Frankly, he looked so appallingly uncomfortable that it was pretty obvious he was lying. Eventually, with a court date imminent, Huhne appeared in front of the media, admitted his guilt and resigned from the government. He was later sent to prison for eight months.

If Huhne had admitted his guilt when the allegation was first made, and apologized, he may well still have had to resign his position in the government. But I doubt he'd have been sent to prison, and it wouldn't have been career-ending. Instead, he chose to lie and lie again, digging himself into an ever deeper hole.

Lying may be tempting under extreme circumstances. But it simply isn't worth it.

That said, and although there are occasions when interviewees have told black lies of the Chris Huhne variety, they are much more likely to offer up false information inadvertently, simply by guessing.

Say, for example, a journalist asks you how much of your company's turnover comes from a particular product line. You might not know, but you want to help the journalist, so you guess: "It's about 15 per cent". But what happens if it's actually 40 per cent, or 3 per cent?

It's important that you tell the journalist if you are not absolutely sure about a piece of information. If you know roughly what the answer is, then you should make it clear to the journalist that you're giving an approximate estimate. And if you don't feel comfortable even giving an approximation, then it's far better to be honest and say that you don't have that figure. If it's a print interview, you can always send the information to the journalist later.

Apologizing

Organizations and public figures often seem terrified of apologizing for anything, as though they'll immediately be damned for doing so. They'll go to any lengths to avoid using the "s" word ("sorry"), and come up with all sorts of euphemisms, the most common of which is "regret". And yet apologizing for something you or your organization has done wrong has two big advantages:

1 It is disarming

As soon as someone apologizes, it dramatically reduces the heat. In contrast, a failure to apologize or a half-hearted apology can make an already-tense situation boil over.

In 2011 Kia Abdullah, novelist and occasional contributor to the *Guardian*, tweeted to her followers that she had "smiled" when she heard that three British students had died in a coach crash in Thailand. Their crime? Two of them had double-barrelled surnames (associated in Britain with what some call the "upper classes"), and they were all on a "gap year" between school and university, which, in Abdullah's eyes, made them rich and privileged enough for their deaths to be celebrated.

Not surprisingly, Abdullah was widely condemned for articulating such a hateful, diabolical and, to the families involved, deeply hurtful thought. But she at least then did the sensible thing. She quickly apologized, stating: "You may not be able to forgive me, but please know that I am truly, genuinely, deeply sorry that I have caused you pain at this time of loss." The storm evaporated instantly, proving that an apology, so long as it is genuine, is the number one tool to get out of trouble fast.

After all, viewers and listeners know that public figures are flesh and blood, just like the rest of us. And if they are open about their mistakes, and genuinely sorry, we forgive them. In his book *Lessons from the Top* (2012), BBC journalist Gavin Esler describes how Bill Clinton survived sex scandals by showing that he was "a repentant sinner". Everyone remembers the Monica Lewinsky scandal, but Clinton would never have made it to the White House without an astonishing confession and apology he made in a 1992 interview on CBS shortly after it had been revealed that he'd been having an affair with the model and actress Gennifer Flowers. What might have been a deal-breaker in Clinton's bid for the White House quickly melted away.

In contrast, a failure to acknowledge failings, personal or organizational, and to apologize, merely serves to fuel a negative story. Early in 2014 it was revealed that a senior British Labour Party politician, Harriet Harman, had worked in the 1970s for an organization with links to the Paedophile Information Exchange (PIE). Harman wasn't the only politician involved, but she's the only one people remember – because the others swiftly apologized. Patricia Hewitt, for example, said: "I got it wrong on PIE and I apologize for having done so".

Harman, however, didn't apologize, possibly because she didn't feel personally responsible for any relationship with the PIE, and therefore didn't see the need to do so. But life isn't always fair, and the story dragged on for days on end. At one stage it looked as though she was doing so much damage to her own party that she'd have to resign. In the end, the story fizzled out, but it would have been extinguished a lot earlier, and done less damage to Harman and her party, if she had simply said "I'm sorry that it happened" right away.

All these examples are about individuals apologizing. But organizations need to apologize too. We'll talk more about this in Chapter 9.

2 It means the journalist has to move on to other topics

The British prime minister David Cameron has had to do his fair share of apologizing. Not surprisingly, he's very good at it. The best example came in the autumn of 2014, shortly after the people of Scotland voted in a referendum to remain part of the United Kingdom. After the vote, Cameron was caught on camera telling former New York mayor Michael Bloomberg that the Queen had "purred down the line" when he phoned her to tell her the result – which would be an insulting expression to use about anyone, let alone the monarch. Asked about it a few days later by the BBC, however, Cameron gave the perfect, damage-limiting response: "I'm extremely sorry and very embarrassed". And he genuinely looked embarrassed too. Since there was nothing more to be gained by pursuing that line of questioning, the journalist swiftly moved on to another topic.

It can be painful to apologize. But the alternative – that your failure to apologize becomes the story of the interview – is more painful still.

Getting your company name into a broadcast interview

Nobody should do an interview just for the sake of it. As we discussed in Chapter 3, you should always have a business objective, even if it's simply "to sell more products". So of course you will want your organization's name to be part of the interview if at all possible.

It's easy to get your name mentioned if the interview is *about your organization* – perhaps an interview about a new product or service you're launching. But it's rather more difficult if you or your spokesperson is being interviewed as an expert on another subject. For example, you might be a partner of a law firm doing an interview about an aspect of intellectual property law, or you might be a spokesperson for an advertising company being asked about the effectiveness of online marketing.

The BBC has always trained its journalists to edit out repeated name drops or blatant advertising from recorded interviews and to discourage them in live interviews. This rule has been followed, to an extent, by commercial broadcasters. So be subtle, or the reporter or presenter will get very irritated. For example, in a BBC Radio 5 Live interview about a new piece of research that had just been carried out, the presenter's first question was about the findings of the research. Unfortunately, the spokesperson's response was: "Well this research, *sponsored by Barclaycard*, was . . .". That was as far as he got before the presenter, and her colleague in the studio, scoffed at such a gratuitous attempt to get the sponsor's name into the story. The interview went downhill from that point onwards.

Almost certainly, your organization will receive a name check when you are introduced at the start of the interview, and you might then attempt, subtly, to get your name into the interview once, or possibly twice, after that. Any more and you're bordering on the gratuitous. These are the ways the spokesperson for an advertising company might do it:

1 By bringing the company name into an example backing up one of the key messages: "For instance, one of our clients at [company name] wanted to do some online marketing in Asia, so we . . ."

2 By using the "We at . . ." formula: "That's why we at [company name] always say to our clients . . ."

As with everything in media interviews, less is often more. So don't be too ambitious, keep it low-key, and only use your company name if it adds to the story. If in doubt, leave it out, and just be satisfied with a name check in the introduction.

Former BBC and LBC presenter Gill Pyrah, now a media-training colleague of mine, says: "It is often to your benefit, as well the broadcaster's, for you to be seen as above the fray and speaking as an expert for your whole industry, not only your company. By implication, your agency, company or brand is being signposted as ahead of the rest in the business. A local radio station will invite the same high street estate agent to comment on movements in home sales whenever national figures are in the news, for example; and the BBC has used the same spokesperson on mortgages for years, name-checking his company at the beginning and end of every interview. His office happens to be only yards from Broadcasting House, but even so, if he'd banged on about his own company in the first interview he wouldn't have been invited back.

"I think one group of interview offenders is the 'in my bookers'. It's so frustrating for a broadcast journalist when an author says:

'That's an amusing story, which I tell in my book'. Of course, they're hoping it will prompt sales but I think the opposite is true: it's a missed opportunity. More than once I've replied: 'But you only have a print run of 5,000 so unfortunately all of the 100,000 or so listening now won't be able to read it.' The author's agenda is to promote his or her book, I get that. But mine is to keep my audience entertained and informed."

As ever, what you're looking for in an interview is the win-win.

Off the record

Off the record can mean different things to different people, so it's important to agree with the journalist what they understand by it before giving any information that isn't strictly *on* the record. But most journalists understand that off-the-record information gives them context to a story, and that, if they want to publish it, they must find another source who is prepared to talk about it *on* the record.

"Unattributable" information is slightly different. If you give a piece of unattributable information to a journalist, then the journalist might well publish it, but won't, or shouldn't, attribute it to you. They might instead refer to "an informed source said . . .", for example, or "a high-ranking official in department X disclosed . . ."

However, using either of these two techniques can be perilous. Former Associated Press journalist Michael Johnson, who has reported in the US, France, Russia and the UK, says: "Some journalists honestly forget which rule they have agreed to, and use the quote as if no restrictions were made. I have been guilty of this more than once. In any case, why would an interviewee want to tell a journalist something that cannot be used? An interview is not a conversation – it's an opportunity to tell your story your way."

Most interviewees on behalf of most organizations will follow Johnson's advice (unless, say, they wish to dish the dirt on a rival). They will never want or need to go off the record, and should have no difficulty sticking to the old adage that you should never say anything to a reporter that you wouldn't be happy to see on the front pages the next day.

Summary

1 Bridging is an essential method for conducting media interviews.

2 Use the helicopter technique to broaden a negative issue out so that it doesn't just focus on your organization.

3 Never avoid a question unless you are happy to be regarded by the viewers and listeners as untrustworthy and slippery.

4 Never say "no comment" unless you want the audience to assume the worst.

5 Within reason, repeat your key messages as often as necessary to make them stand out and be unmissable.

6 Before a live broadcast interview, ask the journalist "How are you thinking of starting?".

7 Accept the fact that you might sometimes be asked unfair questions, and prepare accordingly.

8 Always stick to the truth and nothing but the truth, but don't volunteer negatives.

9 Don't be afraid to apologize if you or your organization has done something wrong.

10 Be subtle about how you bring your organization's name into a broadcast interview.

11 Be wary about going "off the record", and, if you do, make sure you and the journalist agree on the definition.

Exercises

Think about your next interview:

1 Write down your key messages.

2 Predict what kind of questions you might be asked.

3 Create some potential bridges to introduce your messages.

Winning over sceptical and hostile audiences

08

In this chapter we discuss the most effective strategies for conducting issues-based interviews – those where you or your organization hold a particular point of view on an issue of importance, but other people and organizations are sceptical or hold the reverse position. You or your spokesperson's job is to convince the audience to accept and even support your opinion.

For example:

- You are the spokesperson for a construction company, and you need to persuade people that building on greenfield sites will be good for the economy.
- You work for a healthcare organization, and are trying to convince people that junior doctors can and should take on many cases currently handled by their more senior colleagues.
- You are standing for election, and you want people to vote for you.

The spectrum of opinion

Every issue is characterized by a spectrum of opinion (see Figure 8.1). To the right-hand side of the spectrum is your position, while on the left-hand side is the reverse opinion, and your aim should be

FIGURE 8.1 In an issue-based interview, draw your audience towards you

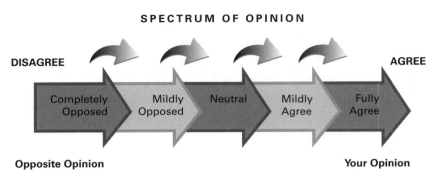

SOURCE copyright Robert Taylor Communications

to draw your audience along the spectrum towards you. It might be too ambitious to think that you could get everyone from the far left all the way along the spectrum to the point where they strongly agree with your position. Not in one interview. But it might still be a "win" for you if you can make people who were completely opposed slightly less opposed, and so on along the spectrum.

But how do you achieve that? Obviously you'll have to have strong messages (or arguments to back up your case). In fact everything we discussed in Chapter 3 about developing strong messages applies to an issues-based interview too. But you are unlikely to win an issues-based interview with strong messages alone, because they typically only allow you to win over people's minds. To win over their hearts, too, the key is to *empathize* with those who feel differently from you on that issue.

To succeed in an issues-based interview, to persuade or convince people, you nearly always need to win their hearts as well as their minds. Yet it's something that so many interviewees neglect.

Bridges of empathy

Imagine you or your spokesperson are doing a TV interview in front of a studio audience on the subject of euthanasia, and you are arguing against its use. Your key message might be that euthanasia is not always in a person's best interests, or that it is not always possible to know whether it's what a patient really wants, and you have plenty of examples and evidence to support your case.

Then, half way through your interview, the journalist invites questions from the audience, and a woman raises her hand and says: "I have a son, aged 23, who is dying from motor neurone disease. Every day, his life is becoming more and more unbearable. He is in constant pain, cannot talk and needs help from a machine just to breathe and swallow. Every morning I pray to God that he'll die that day so that his suffering can be ended. If euthanasia were legal I, his mother, could do what I know he desperately wants me to do, even though he can't tell me, which is to end his life for him. But because of people like you, I can't. Why can't you understand that euthanasia is not a sin, and it's not inhumane, but in cases like my son's, it's an act of love?"

Now, clearly, as a campaigner against euthanasia you are keen to communicate your message as quickly as possible, that euthanasia might not be in a person's best interest. But if you receive that emotionally charged question from a member of the audience and go straight into your key message, you'll look and sound appallingly unsympathetic – not just to the mother but to everyone watching. So what you need to do before you communicate your key message is to build a bridge of empathy with the person who put the question to you.

The more emotionally charged or hostile the question, the bigger the bridge of empathy you need to build. Even with entirely straightforward questions from the audience, you should still build a bridge of empathy. And you should also consider building bridges of empathy with the journalist too if he or she is representing the audience's scepticism or hostility through the tone of their questions.

Examples of short bridges of empathy

- Thank you for that question . . .
- That's a very good question . . .
- Yes, that's an important subject . . .

Such bridges of empathy are useful when someone asks you a purely factual question, with little or no emotional charge, such as: "In how many countries in the world is euthanasia legal?"

Why is even a short bridge of empathy necessary? Because it often takes courage for a member of the audience to ask a question during a live media interview, and they will warm to any interviewee who validates their question in this way.

Examples of medium bridges of empathy

- That's an interesting point of view . . .
- I hear that said quite a lot . . .
- I agree with you on X, but on Y I have to disagree . . .

These medium bridges are useful when the journalist or a member of the studio audience says something which you know to be factually incorrect or is, in your view, an exaggeration. You might respond by saying: "I hear that said quite a lot, but actually the evidence suggests that it is not the case . . ."

Examples of bigger bridges of empathy

- I understand why people feel that way, particularly when they have a family member involved . . .
- Yes, I know that's what some people think, and on the face of it it's a perfectly logical thing to believe, but . . .

These bridges are appropriate when someone (the journalist or a member of the studio audience) asks an overtly hostile question, such as: "You obviously don't care how much dying people suffer, do you?", or an emotionally charged one such as: "Why should I listen to you when by your own admission you've never had a close family member go through this agony?"

So, faced with that emotionally charged question from the mother whose son is dying from motor neurone disease, you'll want to come up with a big bridge of empathy, such as: "I'm so sorry to hear about your son. His situation sounds absolutely awful and my heart goes out to you and your family. Thank you also for asking that question, and my answer is this . . ."

Do such bridges of empathy really make such a big difference? They certainly do – as long as they are sincere and genuine (see below). In fact, unless you empathize genuinely with sceptical, hostile or emotionally charged questions you make your job of winning an issues-based interview much more difficult, if not impossible.

Social psychologist Robert Cialdini offers us some big clues as to why this might be. In his book *Influence: The psychology of persuasion* (1984), Cialdini details his six "key principles of influence", the first of which is "reciprocation". If, as a human being, we receive a favour from someone (perhaps a gift or a compliment) we have a natural urge to return that favour. So, quite simply, if you are faced with an aggressive, emotional and hostile audience (sometimes including a studio audience or callers to a radio programme), and perhaps also an aggressive, emotional and hostile journalist, you can encourage them to listen and consider your point of view simply by empathizing with theirs. They will naturally want to reciprocate.

Many interviewees, particularly those who are most passionate about their cause, often think that if you empathize with people with whom you disagree you merely exhibit weakness or reveal uncertainty about your case. Not so. Empathy is the perfect complement to a strong key message and impressive body language:

- Your key message (backed up, of course, with examples and evidence) wins people's minds;
- Your empathy wins people's hearts.

If you or your spokesperson merely exhibit strong messages the only people who will support you are those who are already inclined to agree with your point of view. But you need strong messages *and* empathy to win over a neutral, sceptical or hostile audience.

Cooling things down

The last thing you should do if you want to convince and persuade people to support your view is to get into an argument. An argument, especially a heated one, just serves the journalist's purposes and those of any viewers or listeners who don't particularly care about who's right or who's wrong but just want to be entertained by the fight. An argument in a media interview is no more likely to serve your purposes, as the interviewee, than an argument in a job interview is likely to win you an employment contract.

So if a journalist, a member of the studio audience or a caller (to a radio programme) targets you with a hostile or cutting comment, try not to meet fire with fire. Instead, give the person what I call a "word-hug" by validating their feelings and showing you understand where they are coming from and why they feel the way they do. Your entirely sympathetic reaction will probably disarm them completely.

As John Neffinger and Matthew Kohut write in their book *Compelling People: The hidden qualities that make us influential* (2014), "Your best hope of persuasion is to keep things non-confrontational, a friendly conversation about a shared problem. Do not let the other side turn it into an argument. Keep everyone's anxiety down and blood pressure low . . . Persevere in being pleasant. Because avoiding the argument is your best chance of winning it."

Yet far too few interviewees seem to understand this. They think they can convince people merely by the strength of their argument and the uncompromising manner in which they communicate it.

In May 2012, one of the leaders of the Animal Liberation Front (ALF), Keith Mann, was interviewed by Stephen Sackur on the BBC's *HARDtalk* programme, which is shown throughout the world. Mann's message was straightforward and strong: that a decent society should value animal life just as it does human life. But right from the start he exhibited no empathy with anyone who might find his movement's often aggressive campaigning methods alienating, and so risked coming across as cold, argumentative and dogmatic.

At one point Sackur asked him about a case in which animal rights activists were jailed for waging a campaign against a family involved in breeding guinea pigs for research. The campaigners had dug up the grave of one of the family who had recently died and said that they wouldn't return the body until the family gave up its guinea pig operations. "Do you think the family were hurt?" Sackur asked. Now, an empathetic interviewee, even one who felt the actions were justified, could have said something like: "I agree they were hurt, and I'm particularly sorry for those members of that family that had nothing to do with farming guinea pigs. However, I do think what the ALF did was justified because . . ." Instead, Mann showed no sympathy at all, and merely repeated the evils that the family was alleged to have propagated.

So Sackur gave Mann another chance to empathize, by detailing exactly what the protesters had done and asking him, "You think that's legitimate, do you?" Mann could have defended the legitimacy, *and still empathized*, by saying: "I understand why people would object to that tactic, and I admit it is extreme and likely to be hurtful, but we felt it was the only way . . ." Instead, Mann replied "Well, it served its purpose."

As a result, and while the interview makes excellent television, which no doubt suited Sackur and the producers of *HARDtalk*, it surely did little to further the cause of the ALF. It is a great example of an interviewee concentrating all his efforts on the force of his argument (ie *what* he was saying) and neglecting warmth and empathy (ie *how* he was saying it).

Those at the extreme end of many issues (and the ALF appear to fall into that category) often find it particularly difficult to communicate with warmth and empathy. Instead, they sometimes communicate with aggression, and even anger, and the more people are alienated by that anger, the angrier they get. It's a self-defeating circle.

Yet it doesn't have to be that way. In December 2009, US animal rights philosopher Tom Regan was interviewed in front of a studio audience on *The Late Late Show* in Ireland. The presenter, Pat Kenny, asked Regan a series of searching and challenging questions, yet Regan empathized beautifully throughout, never getting angry, never getting heated, and always trying to show that there were no easy answers – which a sceptical audience always appreciates. At one point Kenny asked him where he'd draw the line in protecting animals. Would he, for example, seek to protect the life of a wasp? Regan built a textbook bridge of empathy (which I italicize) before going on to his main point: "*I think that is a profoundly difficult question, and I always say wherever you draw the line draw with pencil because you might want to erase it because you find something out that you didn't know before* . . . but where I draw the line is where we have animals with sufficiently good reason to think that they're not only in the world but aware of the world . . ."

As a result of his warmth, empathy and good humour, the audience did Regan the honour of listening to his views and considering them. So much so that when Kenny asked for questions from the audience, the first person to put up his hand (a butcher, no less!) prefaced his question by welcoming Regan to Ireland and thanking him for defying his expectations of what an animal rights campaigner would be like. "You're certainly not what I thought you would be, namely a fundamentalist," the butcher said, with obvious approval. Kenny then listened to the question (about how humans had always eaten meat and therefore always would), and responded with another perfect bridge of empathy: "*First, I want to thank you for your comments, and say that whenever I have a disagreement with a butcher or with any other person who is involved with animals it is never a question of my attacking the person but trying to address the issues themselves.* And so what I think is . . ."

For every subsequent question from the audience, even quite hostile ones, and for some of the questions from Kenny too, Regan built a similar bridge of empathy – thanking the questioner, complimenting them, and pointing out areas of agreement. In fact, if anyone wants a master-class in how to persuade an audience to consider something they might instinctively rail against, they should study Regan's appearance on *The Late Late Show* (Google "Regan Late Late Show Ireland"). It is a wonderful demonstration of empathetic communication with a sceptical audience.

So we have two interviewees, Mann and Regan, both representing the animal rights movement, and both with a similar message, that we must protect the rights of animals just as we do human beings. But whereas Mann's dogmatic communication style is more likely to alienate people than attract them, the strong, determined, passionate, yet softly-spoken and empathetic Regan makes the audience think about and consider his views.

Regan's interview also demonstrates the point made by J Walker Smith, president of Yankelovich Partners Inc, in *Marketing Management* magazine in December 2007: "As the din of voices grows louder, only the softest voices that speak with precision and intelligence will be heard."

Indeed, sometimes the quietest, calmest voices can be the most passionate, powerful and persuasive.

Empathy must be genuine

It is no good learning a few bridges of empathy for each interview and then attempting to shoe-horn them in to your answer whenever you're asked a difficult question. As we saw in Chapter 6, sincerity is a vital component of giving a compelling interview, and your empathy must therefore be genuine.

So take time out before your interview to consider why your opponents don't see it your way, and what makes them hold their beliefs and opinions. Are they just evil? Almost certainly not. Are they just plain wrong? Well, perhaps, but they won't take kindly to being told so. In fact, they probably just have a different way of looking at this particular issue than you do. The more you understand that point of view, and appreciate the motivation behind it, the better able you'll be to build genuine bridges of empathy once the interview starts.

And what if you just cannot find it within yourself to empathize with those who feel differently than you? Simple. Don't do the interview. Hand it over to someone who can empathize. Because if you do it, you'll just end up alienating people who might otherwise be won over to your cause.

Attentive listening

Bridges of empathy are not built with words alone. You can also empathize with the person who is asking you questions by *listening attentively* as they speak. Attentive listening involves two of the three basics of good body language we discussed in Chapter 5:

- Eye contact;
- Posture – ie sitting or standing up straight, with body open and facing the questioner.

It can also involve four others:

- Smiling, when appropriate;
- An occasional agreement word, such as "yes" or "sure" (don't overdo this though, as it will sound like you're interrupting the questioner);
- A short pause for thought before answering, to show that you are considering the point that has been raised and that you regard it as a valid question representing a reasonable point of view;
- Nodding to show that you are listening to the question and understanding the point being made.

Throughout his interview on *The Late Late Show*, Regan was listening attentively to the questions put to him. By doing so he was showing that he was taking those questions seriously, not dismissing them, and that he recognized they were good questions. As a result, he made it much more likely that the audience would listen to and consider his point of view (Cialdini's reciprocation at work).

Clearly, you have to be careful with nodding, because it might look to some members of the audience, whether they are in the studio or watching on TV, that you are agreeing with the premise of the question – and that might not always be the best impression to give. So while it might be a good idea to nod during the first part of the following question, it would be wise not to nod during the second part (in italics): "Those of us in favour of euthanasia just want to keep suffering to a minimum, and to ensure that the families of terminally ill patients can help them end their lives if that's what the patients themselves want. *But those of you who are against euthanasia seem to think that the families of terminally ill patients just want to kill people off. What other logical explanation for your position can you have?*"

It's also worth keeping in mind the age profile of the audience. Older audiences are often more likely to interpret nodding as agreement, whereas younger audiences are more likely to assume it demonstrates understanding of the question or point being made.

Should you go so far as to shake your head during the second part of the question? It's certainly an option, but shaking your head while a question is being asked can look hostile and dismissive – and in order to win people over to your point of view, you must, at all costs, try to take aggression and hostility out of the discussion. (Incidentally, Keith Mann shook his head on occasions during his interview with Stephen Sackur.)

Empathy as a message

Empathy is such an important part of an issues-based interview that, in cases where people feel particularly strongly and emotionally, interviewees might wish to develop it into a full message, complete with examples and/or evidence, which they will try to communicate at the start of the interview.

For instance, an anti-euthanasia campaigner might want to communicate this message of empathy: "I know that pro-euthanasia campaigners have the best motives", backed up by this example: "Anyone who has known someone suffering towards the end of their life knows full well that it can be a ghastly experience, full of physical and emotional anguish. I have a close relative who died of cancer, and her final days were quite simply awful for her and her family, despite the best efforts of her doctors and nurses."

This reaching out to your opponents through a full empathy message also serves to establish common ground upon which everyone, on either side of the debate, can agree. Finding the common ground, the things people can all agree on and cooperate about, is a method frequently and successfully used by arbitrators and mediators.

Tony Blair, for example, writes in his autobiography about how he would try to "set the atmosphere at ease" during what often seemed like intractable disagreements that characterized the Northern Ireland peace negotiations. He would "signify a glimmer of human feeling; exchange a few pleasantries; and above all start by saying something utterly uncontroversial with which disagreement is impossible. Get the other person's head nodding. It's that nod which establishes rapport." All of these things apply to an issues-based media interview too. Take the heat out of the issue, ensuring that people are as open as possible to listening to your point of view.

To return to Pat Kenny's *The Late Late Show* in Ireland, Tom Regan delivered a message right at the start of the interview that was entirely about empathy and finding common ground with his audience. Having thanked Kenny for the opportunity to appear on the show he described how he had been brought up in a "meat and potatoes family" and that during his college days he had worked as a butcher to earn some money to fund his education.

Not only was this initial message entirely about empathy, but it also demonstrated to the audience that he shared a similar life experience with those on the other side of the debate, which was particularly important since he came from another country and might therefore be viewed as an outsider.

This finding of common ground links to another of Cialdini's six key principles of influence: "liking". As Cialdini demonstrates, human beings are more likely to be persuaded by, vote for and buy things from people that they like and who like them. And one of the ways we encourage people to like us is by showing them ways in which we are similar to them, perhaps in our background or interests, or in the way we dress and behave.

In contrast, you or your spokesperson are unlikely to convince anyone about anything if you look, sound and dress as though you come from a different planet.

The "open sandwich" – starting with your example or evidence then hitting the key message

In Chapter 3 we discussed the perfect structure to an answer to a journalist's question: the message sandwich (1. Message; 2. Example/evidence; 3. Message).

However, if your audience is likely to be entirely hostile to your cause, your objective might not be to convince them to support your point of view but simply to make them slightly less hostile. This is the one instance, in any type of media interview, when it might be best to give your examples and/or evidence first, *before* you deliver your message, to ensure that the audience doesn't instinctively shut you out.

Once again, Tom Regan shows how this can be done. He knew full well that the audience on *The Late Late show*, including some who were involved in the meat industry, was likely to be hostile to his key message that animals should be accorded rights just as humans are. So instead of launching straight into that message, he chose first to go into a very personal example of how during the Vietnam War he felt he couldn't support his country in an enterprise which involved, in his words, violence that could not be justified. He then described how impressed he'd been by the teachings of Gandhi, that violence against humans was no different from violence against animals. This had made him think about the meat in his fridge, and whether that too was simply wrong. And finally he got to his key message, that he could see no good reason to justify violence of any sort against animals.

Because he chose to communicate his example first, which the audience would find it easier to accept, they were then much more open to hearing and considering his key message.

Insulting, offending and patronizing people

People feel strongly about things, and when we are trying to argue our point it can be infuriating to be confronted by others who just don't seem to get it or see it our way. It's then that we can be tempted to get aggressive, patronizing and insulting. And yet it's a temptation we should resist at all costs so long as we're in the business of winning over a neutral or sceptical audience to our point of view.

In a British TV debate called *The Big Questions*, an invited audience discusses major ethical and religious questions. In an episode in October 2012 the programme discussed the question "Does God exist?" with an audience that included leading humanists and atheists on one side, and leading religious leaders and other believers on the other. The debate was forceful yet reasonably polite until one of the people representing the non-believers implied that people who believed in God were "idiots". There was uproar in the studio, and outraged cries from all sides. Yet those who were arguing in favour of the existence of God should have been delighted, as such an insulting comment would have served merely to alienate those neutral or undecided viewers from the person who uttered it.

It never ceases to amaze me how just one cutting comment, one moment of lashing out, can blacken an otherwise empathetic tone of voice. I see this all the time during my training courses, particularly when I simulate issues-based interviews in front of a studio audience. And the things that the audience reacts badly to can be quite subtle, and often seemingly insignificant to the interviewee, such as a dismissive gesture, a shake of the head, or a "no, no, that's not the case . . ." It can make all the difference between a win and a loss for the interviewee.

In his book *Emotional Intelligence* (1995), Daniel Goleman, shows how personal attacks, particularly in the form of blanket, generalized statements, can make the person on the receiving end feel helpless and angry. That's undoubtedly true, and even worse, in a media interview, such attacks also make the *audience* feel angry too, because for many of them their natural instinct will be to empathize with the person being attacked.

American pollster and political consultant Frank Luntz, who has covered numerous US and UK elections, has developed mechanisms for tracking people's instinctive reactions as politicians speak, either in set-piece speeches or debates. Covering the UK's first-ever pre-election TV debate in 2010 between the three main party leaders (David Cameron of the Conservatives, Gordon Brown of Labour and Nick Clegg of the Liberal Democrats), Luntz found that "Every time Brown and Cameron went at each other, Nick Clegg was gaining". In other words, bad-mouthing your opponents just drags you both down.

Luntz has also spoken about how US campaigners for greater gun control consistently undermine their own case by insulting their opponents. Speaking at the US PR Summit of 2014, Luntz described an advertisement that the gun-control lobby developed shortly after 20 children were shot dead in Connecticut in 2012. "At that moment," said Luntz, "those who advocated gun control should have won it. But the first ad that they put on the air to promote it showed people with a southern accent sounding and looking really dumb, holding onto their guns. That's so insulting to the millions of Americans who are safe gun owners, the very people you want to reach out to. Even members of the National Rifle Association wanted stricter limits, but when they saw that ad they were so offended about how they were portrayed and they turned away from it."

The lesson here is that aggression and insults tend to turn people off. Yet, over the years, I've heard numerous passionate campaigners for a variety of causes fall prey to the temptation to insult or patronize their opponents. In the field of religion, for example, Richard Dawkins, evolutionary biologist and author of *The God Delusion*, referred to Pope Benedict XVI in media interviews as "Mr Ratzinger", presumably in an attempt to undermine his status and authority. Similarly, in a BBC radio discussion about abortion a pro-choice campaigner referred to a bishop, who was arguing against it, as "a bit of a silly billy". In both cases, listeners registered their dislike of such insults in emails and other messages to the programme. (In the latter case, my instinctive reaction as a listener was to side with the bishop, who ignored the provocation and remained courteous and generous throughout, despite the fact that I felt his message wasn't terribly convincing.)

Of course, if your audience already agrees with you, then there's no problem, from a tactical communications point of view, with insults or patronizing comments towards your common opponent. Winston Churchill used to patronize and belittle Adolf Hitler by referring to him as "Corporal Hitler", and Churchill's audience, of course, lapped it up, because they all shared his opinion of the Nazi leader. And if your sole aim, perhaps in a public election, is to shore up your existing support and encourage them to get to the polling booths and vote, then insults towards your opponents and negative campaigning might well work as a communication tactic.

But if the audience you are trying to convince is in any way undecided or sceptical about your views, empathy is by far the best method of winning them over to your position.

Empathy in politics

Politicians aren't known for their ability to empathize with their opponents' views. And yet, when they do so, they can profit tremendously. Why did so many traditionally Democrat voters support the

Republican candidate Ronald Reagan in the 1980s? At least in part because his values seemed to be theirs. (In fact there were such vast numbers of these voters that commentators coined the term "Reagan Democrat".)

Why was it that so many British Conservative voters switched to voting Labour when Tony Blair was seeking election? At least in part because Blair was so good at empathizing with Conservatives, even convincing some that he was really one of them.

And why was it that the Conservative Boris Johnson was elected Mayor of London, a largely Labour city, not once but twice, defying political arithmetic? At least in part because his infectious humour and charisma appeals to everyone, both on the left and right of the political divide.

The wide world of political communications, in all its forms, is beyond the scope of this book. But politicians would do well to remember that they can gain votes from those who are undecided or open to persuasion by empathizing with, rather than demonizing, their feelings, values and beliefs.

Does empathy work everywhere?

In December 2014 I conducted a media training course in Vienna, attended by delegates from a range of countries including the UK, Ukraine, Serbia, Russia, Germany, Italy and the US. Those from the UK and US quickly recognized the techniques to demonstrate empathy from interviews that they remembered from TV and radio. However, other delegates (especially from Serbia and Russia) said that such techniques were rarely used in their countries, and that audiences didn't expect or require empathy from their politicians and leaders.

So does empathy work only in western cultures, and in interviews on western TV and radio? Of course not. Empathy is a natural human emotion that is not only appropriate in every culture, but is also completely necessary for the functioning of human society.

Just because bridges of empathy are not as yet displayed so often in media interviews in certain parts of the world by no means suggests that they won't be appreciated and reciprocated by audiences in those countries.

To repeat, it would be unethical and possibly counter-productive to *fake* empathy, wherever you are in the world and whatever issue is being discussed. But equally it would be foolish not to demonstrate the empathy that you or your spokesperson genuinely feel. And my experience (I've been lucky enough to train people from all five major continents) shows that genuine bridges of empathy, regardless of culture, are the best way to draw audiences along the spectrum of opinion towards you.

Summary

1 In an issues-based interview, your job is to draw people along the spectrum of opinion towards you.

2 You can do so by building bridges of empathy.

3 The more hostile or emotionally charged the question, the bigger the bridge of empathy that is required.

4 If you want to persuade people to consider your point of view, never get into an argument with the interviewer or member of the studio audience.

5 Make sure your empathy is genuine by challenging yourself to consider why your opponents think the way they do.

6 Attentive listening helps you convey warmth and empathy.

7 When communicating with an overtly hostile or sceptical audience you might want to use empathy as one of your messages . . .

8 . . . and you might want to consider employing the "open sandwich" so as not to alienate them right away.

9 Never insult or patronize those who disagree with you.

10 In politics you can win over undecided voters by empathizing with the way your opponents feel.

Exercises

1 Think of an issue your organization is involved with, and the position you hold on it.

2 What is the reverse position held by other people and other organizations?

3 What sort of hostile or emotionally-charged questions might you be asked?

4 How could you build bridges of empathy with a sceptical audience when discussing your point of view in an interview?

5 How might you demonstrate active listening?

6 Could you develop empathy as a message, and if so, what would you say?

Crisis media interviews

09

What is a crisis interview? To answer that we first need to understand what a crisis is and how it differs from an issue. According to global crisis communications expert Martin Langford, an issue "is characterized by a growing gap between stakeholder expectations and an organization's (in)action. An issue can and often does stand in the way of achieving business results." A crisis, in contrast, nearly always "emerges from an issue that has been mismanaged or not managed at all, and is characterized by sudden, escalating exposure, often via the media." According to Langford, 70 per cent of crises start as issues that an organization either overlooks or mismanages.

So crisis interviews are simply those that take place in the heat of a crisis, and are often regarded as the most adrenaline-pumping of all. Your organization is suddenly under threat. Damage has been done. The media turns hostile and your hard-earned reputation can look very vulnerable.

Yet in many ways handling a crisis interview is simpler than any other. After all, you or your spokesperson don't have to create the story; it's already out there. You don't have to make it newsworthy; it already is. On top of that, there is a simple formula for dealing with crisis interviews, and spokespeople who stick to it typically do just fine and limit the damage to their organization.

How *not* to handle a crisis media interview

Watching badly-handled crisis media interviews is one of the best ways to discover how to do them well. And one interview that has gone down in media-training history about how *not* to do it was given by Lawrence Rawl, chief executive of Exxon Corporation in 1989 after the *Exxon Valdez* oil disaster in Prince William Sound, Alaska. The *Exxon Valdez*, an oil tanker, struck Bligh Reef and spilled millions of gallons of crude oil over the next few days in what is still seen as one of the worst environmental disasters of all time.

In response to the crisis Exxon decided to say as little as possible to the media, which of course just made the media all the more hungry for information and explanation. Finally, after an entire week had gone by, Lawrence Rawl, Exxon's chairman and chief executive, agreed to go live on network TV in the US to defend his company.

This is how the first minute of the interview went:

Presenter: As Charlie mentioned, Exxon released its new clean-up plan as a coalition of groups begin a one-day boycott of Exxon products and several state attorneys general are now calling for a federal investigation into the sharp rise in gasoline prices since the spill. Joining us this morning is the chairman and chief executive of the Exxon Corporation, Lawrence Rawl. Good morning Mr Rawl.

Rawl: Good morning.

Presenter: Can you give me details of this plan. Why was it submitted at the wee hours right before the deadline?

Rawl: Well I can't give you the details of it because as you've indicated, just submitted, this is actually not a new plan, this is a plan for the Gulf of Alaska. The prior plan was for Prince William Sound. So I don't really have all the details. It's a very thick, complicated plan.

Presenter: Well there are some . . . it's not only complicated but some controversy already. You want permission I understand to burn some of the sludge which would circumvent some of the environmental laws. Is that correct?

Rawl: As I just indicated, I don't have all the details, but I'm sure there is a portion of it which indicates that . . . some of the . . . it's not sludge, some of the material that's been picked up or you describe as sludge, burning would be one way of disposing of that, which might require as indicated some relaxation of some air quality. I'm not really familiar with the plan, however.

Presenter: Why aren't you familiar with the plan?

Rawl: Well it was just completed. Obviously there's been some misunderstanding about what a chairman of a world-wide company does, and one of the things you don't do is read every technical plan that is described . . .

Throughout the interview Rawl's body language looked uncomfortable and defensive. Of course, doing a crisis interview is never an easy experience, but it was surely Rawl's attitude to the interview that made it even more uncomfortable for him. Far from being open about what happened, he seemed to have come to the studio to communicate the bare minimum. In any case, he appeared to have very little information to give, perhaps because he had been poorly briefed or because he was concealing things that he did know. Either way, he gave the impression of thinking himself too important to deal with the details of a plan to tackle a massive environmental disaster.

In fact, Rawl committed just about the worst sin you can commit in a crisis interview. He gave the strong impression that he didn't really *care* about the environmental impact of the disaster and the effect on Alaska's wildlife and communities, but *only* cared about protecting and defending Exxon and his position within it.

Once you give that impression, you're on a one-way street to public relations disaster in a crisis situation, which is exactly where Exxon ended up. That applies to any crisis interview on behalf of any organization.

"I'd like my life back"

One might think that today's executives are far too media savvy to get caught out as Lawrence Rawl did in the late 1980s, and turn an environmental disaster into a PR disaster. Well, think again, because today's executives face exactly the same dilemma in a crisis situation as Rawl faced: how much to defend themselves and their organization from mounting criticism.

Take Tony Hayward, former chief executive officer of BP. In April 2010, BP found itself in the middle of a major environmental crisis after the Deepwater Horizon disaster in the Gulf of Mexico, which killed 11 people in what was one of the worst marine oil spills in history. Thrust into the media limelight, Hayward did a series of media interviews, many of which were perfectly fine. But one loose comment in one interview will for ever be remembered and associated with his name. Halfway through a TV interview, Hayward said: "There's no one who wants this thing over more than I do, you know. I'd like my life back." (Google "Tony Hayward life back".)

"I'd like my life back". Understandable on the human level, but catastrophic in PR terms for both him and for BP, because it gave the impression that Hayward cared more about his own life than the lives that had been lost in the disaster, that *he* was somehow the victim, and that he thought *his* life was more important than those of the people living in communities along the coast of Louisiana, for example, which had been devastated.

Is that an unfair assessment of Hayward's thinking and feelings? Yes, almost certainly. But the court of public opinion is often unfair. No wonder that small segment of one interview shot around the world on YouTube and quickly became shorthand for what was seen as BP's inept and uncaring handling of the crisis.

It is easy to have sympathy for Tony Hayward. His life had indeed been turned upside down by the crisis, and as chief executive he was at the very centre of the media storm on both sides of the Atlantic. But in a crisis situation, and however much he was feeling victimized, it would have been far better for Hayward to say nothing about his own life, and just focus on the two most important elements of any crisis interview: concern and action.

A formula for handling crisis interviews

Various formulae have been put forward by crisis communications experts over the years for dealing with crisis interviews, but they have the same fundamental elements. In summary, here are the three steps for dealing with crisis interviews of any sort:

1 Concern/sympathy;

2 Action/explanation;

3 Perspective.

We naturally follow this formula when mini crises strike our own lives. Imagine you've just bought yourself a coffee and a croissant in a crowded café, and, with the coffee and croissant on a tray, you're wending your way through the tables towards one that's free in the far corner. Then disaster strikes halfway across the café. Your left foot clips the edge of a table, unbalancing you. As you lurch forward, the coffee slurps all over the tray and then gushes onto a well-dressed woman in a beautiful white dress.

What's your first response? You immediately say how sorry you are and ask if the woman has been hurt (concern/sympathy). You then explain that you tripped, and you volunteer to pay for the dress to be dry cleaned (explanation/action). Finally, you might explain, with some exasperation and embarrassment, that this is the first time you've ever done such a thing (perspective).

Concern/sympathy

Showing that you *care* about what's happened – that you are genuinely concerned – is the single most important thing to communicate in a crisis interview, especially when people have been hurt, discomforted or, in the worst case, killed. In fact, concern and sympathy are so important that you or your spokesperson should try if at all possible to convey them before you say anything else, because the first words that pass your lips set the tone for the interview as a whole. First impressions matter immensely in a crisis interview.

In the August 2007 edition of *SCT* magazine (McLinden, 2007), crisis communications adviser Gene Grabowski is quoted as saying: "During a crisis step one is always think like a customer . . . 'What do we have to do to alleviate those fears?' If we can get the customer calmed down, then we can calm the media." This is excellent advice, and a good starting point is simply to show the customer that you care about what's happened.

When you express that concern and sympathy, try not to read a prepared statement from your company, or even to sound as though you are doing so. Make it personal. Say what you are *genuinely* feeling about the situation. Speak from your heart.

For example, imagine you are the spokesperson for XYZ Rail Company and one of your trains has just had a crash, killing several people. Your expression of sympathy could be something impersonal and corporate, like this: "XYZ Rail Company would like to extend its sympathy to the families of those who have been killed . . ."

However, that does sound as though you're reading from a press release. Real people don't talk like that. How much more effective, warm and genuine it would be if you or your spokesperson said something far less scripted, such as: "What happened this morning was horrible, and all of us at XYZ were horrified to hear about this crash. I can't imagine what the families of those who have lost their lives are going through, and I send them my heartfelt sympathy."

You'd never read that in a press release, but because of that, and because it comes from the heart, it is so much more effective.

So if Lawrence Rawl of Exxon had his time again, the opening part of his interview might have gone something more like this:

Presenter: Mr Rawl, why was it released at the wee small hours of the morning, right before the deadline?

Rawl: First of all, I'd like to say how appalled I am, as is everyone at Exxon, by what happened to the Valdez oil tanker last week. We know what huge environmental issues this has caused, and we understand very well the terrible impact it's had on the communities in Prince William Sound, and we're going to do everything we can to minimize the damage. Now, you ask about the report, well the reason . . .

US-based communications consultant Margie Elsberg was quoted in the September 2004 edition of *Corporate Legal Times* saying: "If something has gone wrong, acknowledge the truth and look and sound like you care . . . Avoid denying accusations. Denials simply add credibility to the charges." (Flahardy, 2004)

Keeping the tone of concern going throughout your interview

It is not enough to show concern *just* in your first answer. A spokesperson who is genuinely concerned conveys that concern throughout the interview, not just in the opening moments. But how do you do that? You do it by introducing *sympathy words and expressio*ns as the interview progresses. For example:

- Instead of just referring to "the incident", you might want to refer to the "*horrible* incident".

- Instead of just saying that "five people have been killed", you might want to say that "*tragically*, five people have been killed".

- When asked about the lack of available information, you might want to preface your answer by saying something like this: "I know how desperate people are for information at this worrying time . . ."

The important thing here is not to introduce sympathy terms just for the sake of it, or because it's a useful PR tactic. Introduce the kind of sympathy terms that *genuinely reflect the way that you feel*. And, frankly, if you can't bring yourself to feel any concern or sympathy, you shouldn't be doing the interview. Hand it over to someone who does genuinely feel concerned, because they'll do a far better job of it and represent your organization more effectively.

Nearly every spokesperson I've ever trained does feel genuine concern when their organization suffers a crisis. Not concern for the organization (though they might feel that too) but concern for people who have been hurt, frightened, upset or in any way discomforted as a result.

But some spokespeople are better than others at conveying this concern, with the result that some spokespeople who genuinely do care look as though they don't. For example, some people have harsher voices than others, or have sterner expressions, and will therefore have to work even harder at communicating overt sympathy words and expressions than others. Lawrence Rawl of Exxon was definitely among them.

Then there are one or two lucky people who don't have to convey overt sympathy words and phrases at all, so naturally sympathetic do they sound. But they are in a small minority.

The important thing here is to *show* not *tell*. You don't tell the interviewer "I really care", but you show it through your sympathy words and demeanour.

Sympathy words on recorded TV

The other advantage of using sympathy words throughout your interview is that they give you the best chance of coming across as caring in a recorded interview.

Imagine you or your spokesperson are doing a live crisis interview on CNN, which then later plays a recorded segment of that interview (perhaps only 20 or 30 seconds) on a news broadcast. Meanwhile, CNN's website might also carry that 20- or 30-second segment, but not the whole interview. Clearly, you want those few seconds to include at least one sympathy word if at all possible. So as a rule of thumb, try to include one sympathy word for every 20 or 30 seconds of your crisis interview. That gives you the very best chance of conveying the concern and sympathy that you genuinely feel both in the live broadcast *and* in any subsequent recorded broadcasts.

Conveying sympathy in your first answer

Given how important it is to communicate concern in your very first answer, if at all possible, spokespeople need to be ready to think on their feet and ensure that they bridge, if necessary (see Chapter 7), into their expression of concern.

This is easier said than done, especially if the journalist's first question is unhelpful and doesn't lend itself to your conveying concern. But it is so important that you do so, because your first answer sets the tone for the interview as a whole.

For example, in May 1996, a flight operated by US airline ValuJet crashed into the Everglades in Florida shortly after taking off from Miami, killing all 110 people on board. Later that year, the chief executive officer of ValuJet, Lewis Jordan, went on TV in America to discuss the ramifications of the crash. This was the first question put to Jordan by the presenter: "It's been a devastating year for ValuJet both emotionally and financially. Let's start with the financial. How much would you estimate that this crash cost the airline financially?"

That's not an unfair question, because the viewers would no doubt be interested to know about the financial impact of a major crash on an airline. But it was a deeply threatening question, because it invited Jordan to start talking about money before he'd had a chance to talk about the human impact of the crash. Like it or not, that would make Jordan look and sound unsympathetic and callous.

It appears that Jordan was only too well aware of this danger, because he paused slightly after the question was put to him, and glanced upwards as he thought about how to demonstrate where his priorities lay. Then, with a rhetorical twist, he namechecked the human suffering first before going straight on to answer the question about money: "Well our primary focus of course has been on the human side of this tragedy, which was enormous, but from a financial standpoint it's certainly been tens of millions of dollars and it'll be a long time before we know the total cost."

By giving this answer as he did Jordan showed that his heart was in the right place. He was thinking first about the "human side of this tragedy, which was enormous". But he was also respecting the journalist by immediately going on to answering his question about money.

Just as effectively, Jordan then went on to take full responsibility for what happened. This is how the interview proceeded:

Presenter: You've been very up front in this past year about your airline's responsibility in this. How much blame do you take for this crash as an airline?

Jordan: The most difficult question we deal with is that one right there, simply because the FAA [Federal Aviation

Administration] will tell you, the NTSB [National Transportation Safety Board] will tell you, and all the airlines will tell you, you can't delegate safety. We are always responsible for what happens. But one of the things that is not understood is we went to a major contractor and they had done work for big airlines for many years, with FAA-certificated technicians. We checked them out and studied them from a quality assurance standpoint and we chose an agency that was experienced. We didn't take the low bidder. We went with a quality agency that had done good work. We put a quality assurance team in there just like big airlines do, and two big airlines had airplanes in that hangar that same day. And as we oversaw the process something still happened that just continues to say you can never focus too strongly on the safety and the oversight.

This is such a strong, open, honest answer. Jordan explains the situation without making excuses. He takes full responsibility for what happened, while demonstrating that he was personally mortified by the crash. In a few short moments, Jordan demonstrates how to handle a crisis interview.

Why did Jordan accept responsibility for the crash, instead of trying to blame it all on the contractor? Because he knew full well that ordinary Americans, and therefore the media, considered the airline itself to be responsible for safety. The buck didn't stop until it reached the top.

Action/explanation

Whereas concern and sympathy show that you *care* about the situation, action messages and explanations show that you can be trusted to *do something about it*. It's difficult to do a good crisis interview unless it contains both these elements.

In their article Crisis and emergency risk communication as an integrative model in the *Journal of Health Communication* (2005),

Barbara Reynolds and Matthew Seeger describe the importance of action messages and explanation: "Crisis communication seeks to explain the specific event, identify likely consequences and outcomes, and provide specific harm-reducing information to affected communities in an honest, candid, prompt, accurate, and complete manner." In other words, action and explanation (demonstrating how your organization is responding to events) are vital components of a crisis interview.

One of the best examples of a crisis interview involving action messages took place shortly after the Paddington Rail Crash, just outside Paddington Railway station in west London in 1999, in which 31 people lost their lives and 520 people were injured. It was one of the worst rail accidents in British history.

The night after the crash, Railtrack's director of operations, Chris Leah, gave a live crisis TV interview to the BBC at the crash site. This is how it went:

Presenter: The operations director of Railtrack is just across the tracks where the recovery work is being organized. Mr Leah, can you confirm reports that the track-side video shows the driver of the Thames Train going through a red light?

Leah: No I'm afraid I can't confirm that at all. That will be subject to enquiry. But I will say that this is a tragic and horrible accident and I'd like to take this opportunity on behalf of Railtrack and the railway industry to express my condolences and our condolences to the relatives of the bereaved and those who have been injured in this accident, and we will do our utmost to find what went wrong.

Presenter: I gather that your data recorders will have told you by now if the signals were at fault. Can you tell us, and through us millions of your passengers, whether they were?

Leah: The data recorders have been downloaded from the signal box at Slough, and they have been done with Her Majesty's Railway Inspectorate, an outside assessor and the British Transport Police. But I'm not at liberty to say what was in them because the tapes are still in the custody of the police.

Presenter: Can you tell us if the signals were working is there realistically any other likely cause of this accident than a driver driving through a red light?

Leah: I will say that the enquiry and all the investigations will look at all the options and all the other alternatives as to how this horrible accident could occur and there will be no stone unturned. In fact, the deputy prime minister in his announcement this morning said that there would be a public enquiry. Railtrack will play its part to the full in that enquiry.

Presenter: There have been three accidents and one near miss in recent years on this very short stretch of track. What can you say to the thousands of rail passengers who have to use it?

Leah: What I can say is that it is an extremely busy section of line that carries thousands upon thousands of passengers a day. And that we have thousands of very professional and experienced workers both in Railtrack and the train operating companies who day after day, year after year work professionally for a safe industry, and I believe that is what we've got.

Presenter: Mr Leah, thank you very much.

There is much to like about this interview:

- Although Leah's initial expression of sympathy was a little scripted, he did well to communicate it in his very first answer, and then used a sympathy word in his third answer too, when he referred to "this *horrible* accident".

- When he couldn't provide information, he told the journalist why he couldn't (eg the enquiry needs to take place; the tapes are with the police).

- He communicated a series of action messages (eg "we will do our utmost to find out what went wrong"; "the data recorders

have been downloaded from the signal box at Slough";
"Railtrack will play its part to the full in that enquiry").

- He communicated Perspective in his final answer, something we discuss more in a moment.

What a contrast to the crisis interview that Lawrence Rawl of Exxon gave a few years earlier. The big difference is this: whereas Lawrence Rawl's overarching priority seemed to be to defend Exxon, Chris Leah's priority was to communicate openly and honestly. He was putting the interests of passengers and safety ahead of his own corporation, which was exactly the right thing to do – and in the process he served his own corporation better.

"It is too early to say"

Understandably, journalists want to know as much about what happened in a crisis as soon as possible, because that's what their readers, viewers and listeners want. Often that means inviting a spokesperson to speculate or guess about things, such as why the crisis happened, how many people were affected, when it will be resolved and whether it will ever happen again. Yet in the immediate aftermath of a crisis, whether it's a transport-related crash, an IT outage or a financial crisis of some sort, the answers to all such questions may still be unclear.

So how should you or your spokesperson avoid guessing or speculating, which would be dangerous, while still coming across as helpful and open? You do so by using a very simple form of words: "It is too early to say . . ." before bridging to your action messages.

There are lots of variations on "It is too early to say . . ." such as:

- The facts are just emerging . . .
- We need to wait for the results of the investigation . . .
- It would be unwise to speculate . . .
- We must wait for the details to be confirmed . . .

All these expressions effectively say the same thing: "It is too early to say . . ." They allow you or your spokesperson to address the question without speculating or guessing. And as long as you have some good concern and action messages, the journalist will understand and accept your unwillingness to guess or speculate.

Concern and action working together

In their book *Compelling People*, John Neffinger and Matthew Kohut describe a formula to project both strength and warmth in a crisis.

Warmth:

- Validate how people feel – scared, anxious, frustrated, or otherwise;
- Express appropriate remorse;
- Release timely, accurate information to show you are not hiding anything.

Strength:

- Express your determination to fix things;
- Express a clear and thorough understanding of the problem;
- Explain the concrete actions you are taking to fix things.

In other words, you can express warmth through your concern/ sympathy and strength through your action messages and explanations.

Concern and action are therefore the twin pillars of a successful crisis interview. They allow you to communicate with the media even when you don't know much about what's happened. Simply, not knowing all the details is no excuse for a failure to communicate in a crisis. You can *always* do a crisis interview, even when you know very few details, by talking about your concern/sympathy (this is how we feel about it) and your action/explanation (this is what we're doing about it).

US print journalist Sean Wood was quoted in the August 2007 edition of *SCT* magazine saying "the biggest mistake companies can make in dealing with business media is to believe that if they do not talk, nothing will get written." (McLinden, 2007)

Quite right. In a crisis, your instinct might well be to keep your head down and say nothing to the media. That's fine if the media isn't talking about you. But if the media *is* talking about you, communicate, communicate and communicate again.

Michael Bishop of British Midland

In January 1989, a British Midland aircraft crashed onto the M1 motorway in Leicestershire in the UK killing 47 people and injuring 74 others. It was a horrible crisis for the airline, yet the chairman of British Midland, Michael Bishop, was credited for his caring, speedy and authoritative response, which has since been regarded as the textbook way to communicate during a crisis.

Bishop immediately drove to the site of the crash, and made the decision right away to be as open and available to the media as possible, even carrying out interviews on his car phone on his way to the crash site.

Even though he knew little about the causes of the accident, at that stage, and the number of casualties, he told the media what he did know and made it clear that he would let them have any information as soon as he received it.

By responding to the media in such an open and accessible way Bishop communicated his compassion and warmth, but also his authority. Because he demonstrated that the media could trust him, he became the media's main source of information about the crash, and therefore how the story was reported. At the scene, he took personal charge of the operation to support those whose relatives had died and those who were injured. In the middle of the night, he gave a full press conference in which he described how he felt about the accident and the actions that his company had taken.

As a result of Bishop's exemplary handling of the incident, British Midland's ticket sales actually grew after the crash. If ever there was a demonstration of how a crisis doesn't always damage a company, Bishop and British Midland provide it in abundance.

Perspective

If concern and action are the twin pillars of a successful crisis interview, perspective is the optional extra. Perspective is about putting the best light on the situation. For example, if your organization has just suffered a major IT outage that has left you unable to service your customers, you might say:

- This is the first time you've had such an outage;
- Your average service availability is more than 99.9 per cent throughout the year.

The important thing with perspective is not to bring it in too early into your interview. Establish concern first, and then action and only then bring in perspective, otherwise it looks as though your priority is too much about defending your organization and not enough about simply doing the right thing.

In 2008, Willie Walsh, chief executive of British Airways, gave a great demonstration of concern/action/perspective in a BBC interview the day after the catastrophic opening of Terminal 5 at London Heathrow airport, when just about everything that could go wrong did go wrong, with long delays, a suspension of check-in operations and lost baggage. This is how the opening few seconds of the interview went:

Presenter: Willie Walsh, an extraordinary 24 hours. How do you sum it up?

Walsh: Well it definitely wasn't our finest hour. I have to apologize to any of our customers who were disrupted yesterday. We've clearly disappointed a lot of people and I sincerely apologize for that.

Presenter: This was more than teething problems. What on earth went wrong?

Walsh: I think it was a combination of factors. In isolation I don't think any of them would have had the impact we saw yesterday but these factors combined led to problems that we just didn't get control of during the day. Today has started much better. We took a decision yesterday to cancel about 20 per cent of the operation, so it is working better today. And we've got to look to the long term here. This is a fantastic facility. British Airways has not delivered, and we need to deliver. And I'm determined to make this fantastic facility, Terminal 5, I'm determined to make it work.

This is an almost perfect demonstration of a good crisis interview:

1 Concern for those affected, an admission that BA had let people down, and a straightforward apology.

2 An explanation of what happened combined with action messages (eg cancelling 20 per cent of the flights).

3 Perspective: reminding people that Terminal 5 is a great facility, and that Walsh is personally determined to make it work.

Whereas Lawrence Rawl of Exxon tried to deflect responsibility, Willie Walsh accepted it. And what a difference the end result is.

Being ambushed or "doorstepped"

Throughout this book, we've spoken about the importance of thorough preparation for media interviews – preparing your key messages, preparing answers to tricky questions and getting into the right mindset.

But what if you or your spokesperson have no warning at all? What if you're ambushed?

There are usually two reasons why journalists might carry out an ambush interview:

1 They consider it is in the public interest to do so (eg substantial allegations of wrongdoing).

2 The organization in question has failed to respond to interview requests, without good reason.

There's also an unstated third reason: ambush interviews make great TV.

So there's a lot you can do to prevent your organization from becoming the victim of an ambush interview. Global crisis communications expert Martin Langford simply says this about responding to a crisis of any sort: "Communicate, communicate, communicate, with the media and with all your other stakeholders. At all costs, you must resist the temptation to close up and keep your heads down."

Susan Barty, partner at law firm CMS Cameron McKenna, says: "The broadcasting regulations in the UK state that broadcasters should only ambush (or doorstep) in exceptional cases, usually if requests for an interview have been refused. So, to minimize the threat of an ambush, keep the option of an interview open until the very last minute. Try to avoid giving what appears to be a flat refusal."

Clearly codes of conduct and press regulations vary from country to country, but using the British code as a benchmark is a good idea, as British journalists are generally regarded as the most aggressive of all.

So, communicating willingly and genuinely will do much to minimize the risk that a TV crew will want to ambush you. However, if the worst happens and you are ambushed, how should you respond? As ever, one of the best lessons is to look at how *not* to do it.

In 2006, a catastrophic drug trial, operated by Parexel International, took place at Northwick Park Hospital in London. After taking the drug – the first human beings to do so – six healthy young men had a terrible reaction, experiencing huge physical and emotional trauma, suffering organ failure and being admitted to intensive care. Two of them then became even more seriously ill and were later told that they were likely to develop cancer.

Unsatisfied with Parexel International's response to the incident, the UK's Channel 4 *Dispatches* programme decided to ambush Parexel's founder and CEO, Josef H von Rickenbach. The interview (if you can call it that) starts with the Channel 4 reporter approaching von Rickenbach in a hotel lobby, with von Rickenbach looking down at his phone. The interview then proceeds like this:

Reporter:	Mr von Rickenbach?
von Rickenbach:	Yes.
Reporter:	Brian Deer from Channel 4 television in the UK.
von Rickenbach:	Oh, I'm sorry, I'm on the phone.
Reporter:	It's kind of an important matter. I'd like to talk to you about the incident at Northwick Park Hospital where a number of volunteers were seriously injured in a clinical trial operated by your company, sir. [von Rickenbach picks up his bag and starts marching away, pursued by

the reporter.] Do you think I could have a word with you about the incident? [von Rickenbach approaches an official who is sitting down, as though asking what he should do, and then starts marching back across the lobby, again pursued by the reporter.] There's one volunteer Mr Ryan Wilson who has been very seriously injured in a clinical trial run by your company, Mr von Rickenbach. Mr von Rickenbach I do think it's appropriate for you to just stop now and have a conversation with us, about umm. . . . [von Rickenbach pushes through a door and approaches another door.]

von Rickenbach: [Turning over his shoulder towards the reporter.] Look . . . [von Rickenbach shoves the reporter on the shoulder.] Get out of here.

The whole exchange (Google: "Dispatches Channel 4 clinical trial interview") takes only 50 seconds, and yet may well have left these impressions in the minds of the watching public:

- von Rickenbach doesn't *care* about what happened to those young men during the clinical trial;
- He cares only about protecting his reputation;
- His company cannot be trusted.

It is of course possible to feel some sympathy for von Rickenbach. With no warning, he was thrust into an extremely uncomfortable position, and many people would have responded by trying to run away, just as he did. The natural inclination is either fight or flight. Ironically, von Rickenbach ended up doing both.

But how much better would it have been if von Rickenbach had had the coolness not to run away, but actually to speak to the reporter calmly. There were three choices, which, with a cooler head he might have taken:

1 He could have conducted a full interview using the CAP (concern action perspective) formula, starting with an expression of sympathy for the young men involved in the clinical trial.

2 He could have agreed to do a full interview later that day, giving him time to prepare.

3 He could have calmly made a statement while walking towards an area where the reporter couldn't follow, again following the CAP formula.

Any of those strategies would have given him the best chance of leaving these impressions in the minds of the audience:

1 von Rickenbach is taking responsibility for what happened;

2 He cares about what happened;

3 Although that clinical trial went badly wrong, his company can be trusted to respond appropriately.

Later in 2006, the UK's Medicines and Healthcare Products Regulatory Agency (MHRA) issued an interim report on the drugs trial, which showed that Parexel's records and processes appeared in order, including dose measurement and administration, and the MHRA felt that Parexel's actions did not contribute to the serious adverse events. However, von Rickenbach's decision to run away when interviewed gave exactly the reverse impression to TV viewers.

Ambush interviews stack the odds against the spokesperson. It is difficult to come out as a winner, which is why it's important to minimize the risk of an ambush interview occurring. But, should the worst happen, there are ways you or your spokesperson can limit the damage and ways you can intensify the damage. Running away always serves only to do the latter.

Saying sorry in a crisis

Should von Rickenbach have apologized to those young men who took part in the drugs trial? Well, if there is one thing that gets spokespeople tangled up in a moral dilemma it is that very question. On the one side, the spokesperson might well recognize that an apology is warranted, from a purely human point of view. On the other hand, the spokesperson might be worried that an apology will make the organization legally liable for what happened.

The safest way of saying sorry, from a legal point of view, is by using this structure: "We're sorry that [insert incident] happened . . ." Or "We're sorry about [insert incident] . . ." By saying you are sorry that something happened you are no more legally liable for it than you are legally liable for breaking someone's leg if you say: "I'm sorry that you've broken your leg".

But according to Susan Barty, partner at law firm CMS Cameron McKenna, this can be a difficult balance to get right: "The legal implications of an apology are a question of interpretation, but you can minimize the risk of any legal liability by using the formula 'we are sorry that . . .' Also, when you say the 'sorry' or 'we apologize' you should make sure that the context is clear. Make it clear that it does not mean that you are saying you have liability, but merely that you agree, for example, that an awful thing has happened and that you are expressing sympathy to any who have suffered. Also, if the interview is likely to be edited, you need to make sure that the context is clear at all times, to try to reduce the risk of editing being used to suggest responsibility is being accepted."

So if von Rickenbach had conducted an interview, as he should have done, and had been asked by the journalist whether he was going to apologize to the six men involved in the clinical trial, he could have said:

"Of course, I'm sorry about what happened and they have my complete sympathy . . ."
Or:
"Yes I am very sorry that they went through such a horrible ordeal . . ."

In fact, he should have said sorry even if the journalist hadn't asked for an apology.

As we said in Chapter 7, a genuine apology disarms the audience and eases their anger and resentment. Remember, Willie Walsh of BA had no qualms about issuing an apology to his customers during his crisis interview the day after the opening of Heathrow Terminal 5. He knew that an apology was needed and expected, so he gave it without reservation.

Summary

1 In a crisis interview, the most important thing is to show that you care about what has happened. If you don't care, find someone who does to do the interview instead.

2 Remember the simple formula for handling crisis interviews: concern/sympathy – action/explanation – perspective.

3 Try to convey concern/sympathy in your very first answer, setting the tone for the interview as a whole.

4 Introduce "sympathy words and expressions" as the interview progresses.

5 Communicate action messages to demonstrate that your organization can be trusted to respond to the crisis in the most appropriate manner.

6 Avoid speculation by using the expression "It is too early to say . . ." before bridging back to your action messages.

7 Only introduce perspective *after* you have established concern and action.

8 If you are ever caught in an ambush interview, engage with the journalist. Resist the temptation to run away.

9 Don't be frightened of apologizing for what's happened, by saying "I'm sorry that . . ." Apologizing in that way is unlikely to make you legally liable.

Exercises

1 In a worst-case scenario, what kind of crisis is your organization vulnerable to?

2 How might you demonstrate concern/sympathy, action/ explanation, and perspective in a crisis interview?

3 What sympathy words and expressions could you use throughout your interview to keep the tone of concern going?

4 How could you ensure that you or your spokesperson come across as open and honest rather than closed and defensive?

5 What sort of speculative questions might you have to address rather than answer?

6 If you or a spokesperson from your organization were ambushed, how could you engage in an interview rather than running away?

Capitalizing on your interview

10

Once you've completed an interview you will usually have little more influence over what is broadcast or published. Some print journalists will be happy for you to check facts and quotes for accuracy, while others may not, but few journalists worth their salt will allow you to see, let alone comment upon, the full finished version before broadcast or publication.

Nevertheless, there's plenty you can do to capitalize on a good interview and ensure that the next time journalists need comments on a particular subject, they come to you first.

Analyse what went well and not so well

I find it remarkable how often spokespeople say that they don't know how well their interview went because they didn't look at the final result, whether it be a recording of a broadcast interview or the article resulting from a print interview. If an interview is worth doing it's surely worth seeing how it turned out. Otherwise, it'll be very difficult to analyse whether you met your business objective or to improve next time.

So get a copy of the broadcast or publication, and look at it as dispassionately as you can. In his book *Words that Work,* campaigning expert Frank Luntz writes: "It's not what you say, it's what people hear." Very true. So imagine yourself as a viewer, reader or listener. What would they remember from your interview? Would they do something differently as a result? It is also worth asking a colleague or friend to review the interview and provide feedback as to the main message that they took away from the article.

When listening to a recording of a broadcast interview, consider these points:

- Did your or your spokesperson's key messages come over clearly? If you've done your job properly, your messages should have been unmissable.

- Were your messages backed up with strong examples and evidence? Remember, a message is unlikely to be remembered or acted upon by your audience unless it is supported by strong proof points.

- Did you answer or at least address every question before bridging back to your key messages? Ideally, your messages will have dominated the interview.

- Was your tone of voice W.I.S.E. (Warm, Intelligent, Sincere and Enthusiastic/Empathetic)? Without a good tone of voice, your audience is unlikely to remember and act on your key messages.

- Did your pace of delivery allow your audience time not just to hear every word, but to digest every word – particularly your key messages? It's no good gabbling through your messages so fast that nobody notices them.

- For TV, was your eye contact good, and was your posture straight and relaxed? Without good body language, your content won't convince anyone.

When reviewing an article resulting from a print interview, ask yourself:

- Was anything you or your spokesperson said taken out of context or given more prominence than you had intended?

- Would an average reader remember and act upon your key messages?

- Do your examples and evidence support your key messages?

And most importantly of all, for any interview, *did you meet your business objective*? In other words, did you give yourself the best chance of convincing the audience to do what you wanted them to do?

If you or your spokesperson are honest about what went well and what could have gone better you'll give yourself the best chance of improving your performance next time.

Use social media to ensure your interview is seen, heard or read by your target publics

The reason you do an interview is to influence your target audiences and to encourage them to act in a way that will help you and your organization. So don't just leave it to chance whether your target publics hear, see or read the interview. Make sure they do. You should, for example:

- Tweet about the interview before it is broadcast or published.
- Tweet a link to the interview once it's online.
- Retweet any favourable comments about it.
- Write a blog about its subject matter.
- Include a link to your interview in your organization's newsletter and on its website.
- Email a recording of the broadcast or a copy of the article directly to your customers (and others).
- Consider playing a recording of any broadcast interview you do at customer events or at exhibitions.

Digital media expert Edd Withers says: "If the publication has tweeted a link to your interview don't forget to retweet it. This will ensure the story is placed into your followers' news feed from an independent point of view, which will give it greater credibility. If you have a blog, you could publish a blog with the interview quoted, or if it's a recorded interview you could embed the video or sound clip directly into the blog. Perhaps you have a mailing list or newsletter. Again, use this to publicize your successful interview to capitalize on its message.

"Don't forget to monitor social media throughout the transmission and in the days after. Keep searching for your name on social media channels, to judge how the interview has been received, and also to estimate the effective reach of the interview with that particular organization."

Social media strategist Andy Black adds: "Consider adding a link to the video interview in your LinkedIn profile. This will enhance your profile and professional image to your current and future LinkedIn connections. You can also share a link to the video interview in LinkedIn, and this will appear in the news feeds of your connections. If your connections operate in multiple time zones, there is no reason why you can't share the link many times with a different title or description over a short period of time. Consider using a scheduling tool to assist this process. You can also send a private message to all key LinkedIn connections with the link and a personal message. Also consider using the link in paid LinkedIn ads as you can target the ad to executives with specific job titles in specific companies. A similar strategy can be used for Twitter, Facebook and Google+ for both video and audio interviews."

There's no doubt that social media offers a huge range of possibilities for making sure that your interview reaches your target audience. And most of them bypass journalists altogether – just look at the popularity of the AMA (Ask Me Anything) feature on reddit.com, which has been used by some of the most famous names in the world including Barack Obama, Bill Gates and Madonna. In fact, interviewees could consider doing an AMA to follow up on an interview they have already conducted with the traditional media.

And if you don't like something the journalist wrote?

In most cases you'll be well advised not to complain to the journalist, though it might be worth your while pointing it out, as diplomatically as possible, in a polite email or phone call. And you should certainly mention any factual errors if only to ensure that the journalist doesn't make the same mistakes again.

Only use the nuclear option, of demanding a published apology or correction, for something that will have a seriously damaging impact upon your reputation or that of your organization. After all, the journalist might be a valuable contact for you, and you don't want to ruin that budding relationship by complaining about something relatively insignificant.

Build a strong relationship with the journalist

All journalists need spokespeople who are willing and available to be interviewed. So keep in contact with the journalist so that you are front of mind when they write another article that needs contributors. For example:

- Send a note to thank them for the interview and make a few helpful and supportive comments about the final broadcast or article.

- Put them on your organization's mailing list for newsletters or reports (ask first of course).

- Follow them on Twitter and Facebook, and suggest that they follow you.

- Retweet and Favourite the journalist's postings on Twitter.

- Where appropriate (and don't over-do this) contact the journalist to let them know of other stories or subjects you could comment on.

- Tell the journalist about other contacts of yours, including clients, who might make suitable interviewees (check with those contacts and clients first, of course!).

- Send the journalist any articles or blogs you've read that you think might be of interest.

- Invite the journalist to events your organization is holding.

- Be prompt in returning calls and responding to emails, and go out of your way to be available when the journalist wants to interview you again.

In other words, treat the journalist as you would a valued client, and ensure that you maintain a strong mutually beneficial relationship.

Summary

1 Make sure you see the results of your interview. For a broadcast interview, get a recording. For a print interview, get a copy of the published article.

2 Look at the final product through the eyes of the reader, viewer or listener, and analyse what went right and what could have gone better.

3 Ask yourself whether you met your business objective, and if not why not.

4 Use social media to ensure your interview is seen, heard or read by your target publics.

5 Build a relationship with the journalist and treat them as you would a client.

Exercises

1 Consider a recent interview you or your spokesperson gave to a journalist. What went well and what could have gone better?

2 Did you achieve your business objective?

3 How might you use social media to maximize the impact of your interview?

4 How might you build a strong relationship with the journalist to maximize your chances of being asked to do further interviews?

BIBLIOGRAPHY

Blair, T (2010) *A Journey,* Hutchinson, London

Brice, S (2003) "Who's that talking in my earpiece?": the art of doing a remote interview, *Tactics* magazine, **10** (5) (May), p 21

Chaney, P (2012) Word of mouth still most trusted resource says Nielsen; implications for social commerce, *Digital Intelligence Today*, 16 April [Online] http://digitalintelligencetoday.com/word-of-mouth-still-most -trusted-resource-says-nielsen-implications-for-social-commerce/ [accessed 3 April 2015]

Cialdini, R (1984) *Influence: The psychology of persuasion,* HarperCollins, New York

Davies, P (1994) *Total Confidence,* Piatkus, London

Duarte, N (2010) *Resonate*, John Wiley & Sons, Hoboken

Engel, P (2014) Here are the most- and least-trusted news outlets in America, *Business Insider,* 21 October [Online] http://www. businessinsider.com/here-are-the-most-and-least-trusted-news-outlets- in-america-2014-10#ixzz3YmpzcmcO [accessed 3 April 2015]

Esler, G (2012) *Lessons from the Top*, Profile Books Ltd, London

Flahardy, C (2004) Attendees learn how to weather a media firestorm, *Corporate Legal Times*, **14** (154) (September), p 58

Friedman, K (2005) How to shine in the media spotlight: a former reporter reveals the secrets of successful spokespeople, *Marketing Communications,* **22** (3) (May–June), pp 37–44

Frohlichstein, T (2003) Follow me: message maps lead the way to better media interviews, *Tactics* magazine, **10** (5) (May), p 20

Gibson, B (2008) Spokespeople: be authentic – lose the overscripted Q&A doc, *Marketing Communications*, available from https://www.iabc.com/ wp-content/uploads/2014/10/In-My-Opinion7.pdf

Goleman, D (1995) *Emotional Intelligence*, Bantam Books, London

Hamermesh, D (2004) Maximizing the substance in the soundbite: a media guide for economists, *Journal of Economic Education,* **35** (4) (Fall), pp 370–82

Harcup, T and O'Neil, D (2001) What is news? Galtung and Ruge revisited, *Journalism Studies* **2** (2), pp 261–80

Howard, C (2002) Polishing your spokesperson skills for news interviews, *Public Relations Quarterly,* **47** (4) (Winter), pp 18–20

Hudson, G and Rowlands, S (2007) *The Broadcast Journalism Handbook*, Pearson, Harlow

Jensen, P (1997) Evolution and revolution in child psychiatry: ADHD as a disorder of adaptation, *Journal of the American Academy of Child and Adolescent Psychiatry*, **36** (12) (December), pp 1672–79

Luntz, F (2007) *Words that Work*, Hyperion, New York

Marr, A (2004) *My Trade: A short history of British journalism*, Macmillan, London

McLinden, S (2007) Are you prepared to meet the press? *Shopping Centers Today*, **28** (8) (August), p 66

Mehrabian, A and Wiener, M (1967) Decoding of inconsistent communications, *Journal of Personality and Social Psychology*, **6** (1) (May), pp 109–14

Milne, S (2008) In touch: comment on the art of the sound bite, *Management Magazine*, (February), p 13

Morgan, P (2010) When Piers met Nick Clegg, *GQ Magazine*, 23 July [Online] http://www.gq-magazine.co.uk/comment/articles/2010-07/23/when-piers-met-nick-clegg

Neal, D and Chartrand, T (2011) Embodied emotion perception: amplifying and dampening facial feedback modulates emotion perception accuracy, *Social Psychological and Personality Science*, **2** (6) (November), pp 673–78

Neffinger, J and Kohut, M (2014) *Compelling People: The hidden qualities that make us influential*, Piatkus, London

Pape, S and Featherstone, S (2005) *Newspaper Journalism: A practical introduction*, SAGE, London

Phillips, A (2007) *Good Writing for Journalists*, SAGE, London

Phillips, B (2007) Don't alienate your audience: injecting passion into your information and anecdotes for a winning combination, *Tactics* magazine, **14** (5) (May), p 15

Reynolds, B and Seeger, M (2005) Crisis and emergency risk communication as an integrative model, *Journal of Health Communication*, **10** (1) (Jan–Feb), pp 43-55, available at http://journals.taylorandfrancis.com/forms/hcm/10_43.pdf

Rosenbaum, C (2007) Friendly persuasion: how to excel in media interviews, *Tactics* magazine, 29 November, available at http://www.prsa.org/SearchResults/view/1453/105/Friendly_persuasion_How_to_excel_in_media_intervie#.VY1A5PlVhBc

Rouder, J, Morey, R, Cowan, N, Zwilling, E, Morey, C and Pratte, M (2008) An assessment of fixed-capacity models of visual working memory, *Proceedings of the National Academy of Sciences of the United States of America*, **105** (16), pp 5975–79, available at http://www.pnas.org/content/105/16/5975.abstract?tab=author-info

Salt, B (2012) How they cut dialogue scenes, *Cinemetrics* [Online] http://www.cinemetrics.lv/dev/cutdial.php [accessed 20 November 2014]

Smudde, P (2004) The five P's for media interviews, *Public Relations Quarterly,* **49** (2) (summer), pp 29–34

Sommers, S (2009) Full court press: managing media interviews, *Tactics* magazine, **16** (3) (March), p 19

Thaler, R and Sunstein, C (2008) *Nudge*, Yale University Press, New Haven CT

Tidmarsh, A (2014) *Genre: A guide to writing for stage and screen*, Bloomsbury Methuen Drama, London

Walker Smith, J (2007) New ways of talking, *Marketing Management*, **16** (6) (November/December), p 52, American Marketing Association

Wanjek, C (2013) Left brain vs. right: it's a myth, research finds, *livescience*, 3 September [Online] http://www.livescience.com/39373-left-brain-right-brain-myth.html [accessed 13 December 2015]

Work, S (n/d) How loading time affects your bottom line, *Kissmetrics* [Online] https://blog.kissmetrics.com/loading-time/ [accessed 30 November 2014]

INDEX

Note: the Index is filed in alphabetical, word-by-word order. Headings in *italics* denote document or programme titles; numbers within main headings are filed as spelt out and acronyms are filed as presented. Page locators in *italics* denote information contained within a Figure or box; locators as roman numerals denote material contained within the Foreword.

ABC
  bridging technique 15, 71, 122, 127–30, 138–40, 150, 194
    news channel 72, 74, 111
Abdullah, Kia 145–46
accepting media interviews 1–8, 10
achievement listing 64
acronyms 112
action 172, 173, 178–83, 185, 190
  calls to 53–54
action-orientated objectives 27–29
actions, negative 29
addressing questions 128, 134, 180, 194
  see also answers
adrenaline 61–62, 65, 92, 99, 169
  see also anger; over-confidence
advertising (adverts) 2, 3, 31, 34, 64, 147–48, 164
aeronautical analogies 41
aerospace industry 112
Africa 92
age profile, audience 160
aggression 157, 161, 165
  see also anger; insults
agreement words 160
Air Transport 112
AMA 196
ambushing 185–89, 190
analogies 41, 58
analysis 193–95, 198
Anderson, Dr Jeff 45
Andrew Marr show 78
  see also Marr, Andrew
anger 72–78
  see also aggression; arguments; insults
animal rights messages 156–59, 162–63
answers 33, 44, 72, 128, 129, 134, 176–78, 194
  fleshing out 120–22, 124

  see also messages; questions
apologizing 145–47, 150, 185, 188–89, 190, 197
approximations 144–45
Archer, Jeffrey 48–49
arguments 155–59, 167
  see also insults
Armstrong, Neil 47
Ask Me Anything 196
assertiveness 61, 72, 74, 83
asthma treatment messages 130
attentive listening 159–61, 167
audiences 1–2, 6, 12, 107, 110–12, 124, 151–68
  and message reception 29–30, 32, 43, 49–50, 51–54
authors 148–49
avoiding questions 105, 131–37, 150

bad news 4–5, 6–8
Balding, Clare 17
Bartlett, Jamie 71–72
Bashir, Martin 35
basic information (questions) 12–13, 26
Bates, Stephen 134–37
BBC 1, 2, 17, 75, 109, 111, 123, 129, 139, 165
  Heathrow Airport Terminal opening 184–85
  Paddington Rail disaster interview (1999) 179–80
  Radio 4 14-16
  Radio 5 Live 70, 147–48
  see also Bashir, Martin; *Breakfast TV*; Bruce, Fiona; Esler, Gavin; *HARDtalk*; Marr, Andrew; *Match of the Day*; *Newsnight*; Paxman, Jeremy; Pyrah, Gill; Radio 5 Live; *Today Programme*; Vine, Jeremy
Beckham, David 95

behaviour
    offensive 163–65
    patronizing 163–65, 167
Bennett, Natalie 95–98
Big Questions, The 163–64
bigger bridges of empathy 154–55
Bishop, Michael 183
BlackBerry Ltd 134–37
    see also Research in Motion
Blair, Tony 16, 18, 35, 93, 161, 166
blogs 195
Bloom, Godfrey 75–76
body language 85–90, 92–93, 99, 101,
        171, 194
    see also nodding; shaking head
BP 9, 172
brain system development 51
brand, organization 100
Breakfast TV 70, 71
breathing 61–62
    exercises 67–68, 83
bridges of empathy 152–55, 158,
        166–67
bridging 15, 71, 122, 127–30, 138–40,
        150, 194
    see also bridges of empathy
British Midland 183
broadcast interviews 46, 57, 62, 68–78,
        80–82, 107, 111, 148–49
    live 83, 140–41, 150
    recorded 83, 176
Broadcast Journalism Handbook, The,
        (Hudson & Rowlands) 63, 106
Brown, Gordon 93, 115, 133, 164
Bruce, Fiona 78
Bush
    President George, H W 48
    President George W 16–17, 18
business
    objectives 27–31, 32–33, 58,
        194–95, 198
    stories 5

Caborn, Richard 17, 18
calls to action 53–54
Cameron, David 18–19, 90, 134, 146–47, 164
Campbell, Alastair 61–62, 63
'car crash' interviews xii
car industry 105
cautious responses 72
caving technique 131
change 6
charismatic hang out 119
Churchill, Winston 165
Clark, Gabriel 77

Clarke, Ken 75
Clegg, Nick 134, 164
Clinton
    Bill 115, 146
    Hillary 41
Cluley, Graham 111
CNN 1, 111
colour 118–19
commercial business objectives 28
common ground 161
communication 128–30, 179, 182–83, 185
    tactics 165
    see also answers; conversational delivery;
        corporate speak; messages
company names 148–49, 150
*Compelling People: hidden qualities that
        makes us influential, The* (Neffinger
        & Kohut) 156, 182
complaints 196–97
concentration 69
concern 172–78, 182–83, 190
confidence boosting 63–68, 71, 90
    see also over-confidence
confidential information 40
control, interview 127–50
controlled passion 77, 83
conversational delivery 107–17, 124
copy, interview 193–94
core messages 29
corporate
    script 20
    speak 107–09
Costolo, Dick 35
Crick, Michael 75–76
crisis, defined 169
    media interviews 169–91
curtness 120–22

damage, to organization 9
Davison, Ruth 115–17
Dawkins, Richard 165
declining media interviews 8–10
Deepwater Horizon disaster 172
defensive messages 33, 171–72, 181
delivery pace 90–92, 194
denials 175
Derbyshire, Victoria 75
Diana, Princess of Wales 35
Dispatches 186–88
doorstepping 185–89
down-the-line interviews 87–88, 101
dress sense 99–101
dressing the set 23
Dubai 40
Dukakis, Michael 76–77

ecology messages 109–10
editorial information 2
education messages 48–49, *55*, 107–09, 113,
    117–18
emails 195, 197
emotion 66, 118–19
empathy 105–06, 119, 152–55, 156–59,
    161–62, 165–67
  of audience 164
energized delivery 92
enthusiasm 94, 105, 106, 110, 119
environmental disaster messages
    170–72, 174
errors, factual 196–97
Esler, Gavin 22–23, 38
ethics 40, 76, 80, 167
euthanasia messages 152–55, 160, 161
Everington, Dr Sam 129–30
evidence 37, 43–45, 49, 53, 58, 105,
    124, 194
examples 36, 37–43, 44–45, 49, 53, 58, 105,
    124, 194
expertise 8, 64, 83, 147
explanation (action) 172, 173, 178–83,
    185, 190
explanations 36–37
expressive language 118
Exxon 170–71
eye contact 86–88, 122, 159, 194

factual errors 196–97
fake
  empathy 167
  (forced) smiles 93, 101
Falkland Islands 38–39, 43, 138–39
Ferguson, Sir Alex 77–78
filler words (sounds) 94–98, 101
films 52
final messages 53–54
financial messages 19, 57
first
  answers 72, 176–78
  questions 18, 70, 72, 132, 133,
    140–41
five P's 69
fleshing out answers 120–22, 124
focus 70
'For the many not the few' *35*, 37
forced marriages 39
Fox News 111

general knowledge questions 16–19
generalizations 164
*Genre: A guide to writing for stage and
    screen* (Tidmarsh) 42

gestures 92–93, 101
'Give me the proof' 36–45
Global Trust in Advertising (2012) 2
GMTV 70
GQ Magazine 134
graphic language 118–19
great
  messages *35*
  news 6–8
Griffin, Merv 114
guarantees 142
guessing 144–45
gun-control messages 164–65

HARDtalk 156–57
Harman, Harriet 146
Hayward, Tony 47, 172
head, shaking 160–61
headlines 50–51
  see also key messages
helicopter technique 130–31, 150
Hewitt, Patricia 146
high-definition TV 101
Hiller, Andy 16–17
Hoddle, Glenn 79
'home base' 29
home economics questions 18
honesty 143–45
horsemeat scandal (2013) 123
hostile
  audiences 151–68
  questions 14–16, 75
hotel chain key messages 30
Howard, Michael 132
Huhne, Chris 144
humour 122–24, 124
Humphrys, John 69–70, 115–16
hyperventilation 61–62
hypothetical
  mind pictures 40–41
  questions 142

IATA 112
Iceland (supermarket) 123
ICO 22
'I'd like my life back' 171–73
impossible guarantees 142
industry topics 20–21, 26
  see also car industry; IT industry;
    manufacturing industry; oil industry;
    retail industry
*Influence: psychology of persuasion,
    The,* (Cialdini) 155
influence, key principles of
    155, 162

information 24
    basic 12–13, 26
    confidential 40
    editorial 2
    off the record 149, 150
    organizational 19–20, 26
    unattributable 149
insincerity 104–05
    see also sincerity
insults 163–65, 167
    see also arguments
intelligent voice tone 104, 110
International Air Transport Association
    112
International Financial Law Review 110
interruptions 87
interviews
    accepting 1–8, 10
    'car crash' xii
    control of 127–50
    copy 193–94
    declining 8–10
    down the line 87–88, 101
    issues-based 151–68
    length 46, 57
    links 195, 196
    notes 54–56, 58, 98–99
    phone 90
    practice 14, 21, 24–25, 65, 83, 99, 122
    print 46, 62, 78–79, 83, 107, 111–12,
        113, 198
    simulated 24
    sit-down 89–90
    Skype 87
    stand-up 88–89
    TV 22–23, 26, 56, 98, 99–101, 176
    video 56
    see also broadcast interviews
Irish Food Standards Agency 123
issue, defined 169
issues-based interviews 151–68
IT
    business objectives 28
    industry 41
'it's too early to say' 181–82, 190

jargon 107–09, 112–13, 124
Johnson
    Boris 41, 123–24, 166
    Michael 45, 80, 149
Jordan, Lewis 177–78
journalists 3, 7, 9, 12, 57–58, 62, 63–64,
        72–76, 83, 141
    building relationships with 197–98, 198
    and doorstepping 185–89

dress 100
errors and complaint handling 196–97
and media training 25–26
and message creation 31–45, 47, 50–51
and off the record information 149
and PR departments 21
    see also Balding, Clare; Bashir, Martin;
        Bruce, Fiona; Campbell, Alastair;
        Clark, Gabriel;
        Crick, Michael; Derbyshire, Victoria;
        Hiller, Andy; Humphrys, John;
        Johnson, Michael;
        Lewis, Martin; Marr, Andrew;
        Morgan, Piers; Parris, Matthew;
        Paxman, Jeremy; Sackur,
        Stephen; Shaw, Bernard

Kennedy, John 47
Kenny, Pat 157–59
key
    messages 27, 29–45, 46, 50, 55, 58, 91,
        138–40, 150
    analysis of 194
    scripted 20
    see also top-line messages
    principles of influence 155, 162

Labour Party 35, 37
language
    body 85–90, 92–93, 99, 101, 171, 194
    conversational 113–17
    expressive 118
    graphic 118–19
    see also jargon; legal terminology;
        specialist terminology
Late Late Show, The 157–58, 160,
        162, 163
Lazaridis, Mike 75
LBC 65, 95–98
Leah, Chris 179–81
legal
    departments 20
    terminology 110–11
Lessons from the Top (Essler) 22, 38, 146
Lewis, Martin 94, 118–19
liability 188–89
liking 162
line, organizational 19–20, 26
LinkedIn 196
links, interview 195, 196
listening 159–61, 167
live broadcast interviews 83, 140–41,
        150
Luntz, Frank 164–65, 193
lying 105, 144

Mair, Eddie 14–16
make up 100
Mandela, Nelson 90–91
Mandelson, Peter 139
Mann, Keith 156–57, 161
manufacturing industry 29, 120–22
Marr, Andrew 3, 57, 61, 63, 78
marriages, forced 39
Marsh, Steve 70–71
Match of the Day 77
material, confidence in 71
Maude, Francis 14–16
media
    social 48, 195–96, 198
    training 24–26
medium bridges of empathy 154
message sandwich structure 45–50, 58, 122,
        124, 162–63, 167
messages 94
    animal rights 156–59, 162–63
    asthma treatment 130
    communication 128–30
    control 8–9
    core 29
    creation 27–59
    defensive 33, 171–72, 181
    ecology 109–10
    education 48–49, 55, 107–09, 113,
        117–18
    empathy 161–62
    environmental disaster 170–72,
        174
    euthanasia 152–55, 160, 161
    final 53–54
    financial 19, 57
    great 35
    gun-control 164–65
    menu 56–57
    message sandwich structure 45–50, 58,
        122, 124, 162–63, 167
    mind map of 56–57
    prison reform 48–49
    remembering 54–58
    scripted 20
    self-explanatory 37
    seven word 34
    smoking 129–30
    stress-testing 24
    sub-messages 29, 30, 31
    supercharged 34
    technology 30–31, 111, 184
    10 word 33–36, 46, 53, 58
    top-line 34–35, 44–45, 49, 56
    university 30, 131
    see also key messages

metaphors 41
Miliband, Ed 89, 139
mind
    map 56–57
    pictures 38–40, 40–41, 49, 56, 57, 58,
        110, 117–19, 124
Mind Tools 64
mistakes 88
mobile technology 43
Morgan, Piers 134
Motson, John 77

Naughtie, James 7
negative
    actions 29
    questions 135, 137, 142
    stories 8
    summaries 142
negatives, repeating 143
nervous ticks 99
nervousness 61–72
neuro-linguistic programming (NLP) 65
news stories 2–8
Newsnight 41
niche (target) audiences 110–12
Nixon, Richard 47, 143
'no comment' 21, 137–38, 150
'no' questions 142
nodding 160, 161
Northwick Park Hospital drugs trial 186–89
notes 54–56, 58, 98–99
    'thank you' 197
NPR 2
Nudge (Thaler and Sunstein) 44
numbers, as evidence 43–44

objectives 27–31, 32–33, 58, 194–95, 198
obvious questions 14–16
off the record information 149, 150
offensive behaviour 163–65
oil industry 41, 131
    see also BP; Exxon
open sandwich message structure
        162–63, 167
opinion, spectrum of 151–52
opposite (reverse) opinion 151–52
organization
    brand 100
    damage 9
    defence 33, 171–72, 181
    information 19–20, 26
    liability 188–89
    line 19–20, 26
    see also company names; corporate script;
        corporate speak

Ortmann, Max ('Mad Max') 72–74
over-confidence 78–82
    see also preparation
over-repetition 139
own words usage 20

pace of delivery 90–92, 194
Packaging World Magazine 2
Paddington Rail crash (1999) 179–81
Pakistan 41
Parris, Matthew 133
passion 61, 77, 86, 90, 101, 110, 155,
    158–59
    controlled 83
passive smoking messages 129–30
patronizing behaviour 163–65, 167
pausing 91, 92, 101, 160, 177
Paxman, Jeremy 132
PBS 2
Perceptual Positions 65
personality 118–19
perspective 173, 181, 183–85, 190
Pew Research Centre 2
Philip, Prince 78
phone interviews 90
pictures, mind 38–40, 40–41, 49, 56, 57, 58,
    110, 117–19, 124
Player, Gary 65
politicians 113–17, 131–32, 133, 134,
    165–66
    see also Archer, Jeffrey; Bennett, Natalie;
    Blair, Tony; Bloom, Godfrey; Brown,
    Gordon;
    Bush, President George H W; Bush,
    President George W; Caborn,
    Richard; Cameron,
    David; Churchill, Winston; Clarke, Ken;
    Clegg, Nick; Clinton, Bill, Clinton,
    Hillary;
    Dukakis, Michael; Harman, Harriet;
    Hewitt, Patricia; Howard, Michael;
    Huhne, Chris;
    Johnson, Boris; Kennedy, John;
    Mandela, Nelson; Mandelson, Peter;
    Maude, Francis;
    Miliband, Ed; Nixon, Richard;
    Ortmann, Max; Prescott, John;
    Reagan, Ronald; Roosevelt,
    Franklin D; Ruddock, Philip; Smith,
    Chloe; Thatcher, Margaret; Zardari,
    Asif Ali
posture 88–90, 101, 159, 194
PR departments 19–20, 21–23, 104
practice interviews 14, 21, 24–25, 65, 83,
    99, 122

preparation 11–26, 44–45, 56–57, 65, 69,
    70–71, 72, 98
prepared statements 8–9, 174
Prescott, John 77
pressure handling 68–72
print interviews 46, 62, 78–79, 83, 107,
    111–12, 113, 198
prison reform message 48–49
prompt words 56
proof 36–45
provocation 70
publicity 9
published apologies 197
Pyrah, Gill 34, 63–64, 65, 100–01, 148

questions 12, 13–19, 21, 26
    addressing 128, 134, 180, 194
    avoiding 105, 131–37, 150
    'damned either way' 142
    first 18, 70, 72, 132, 133, 140–41
    hostile 75
    hypothetical 142
    negative 135, 137, 142
    unfair 76–77, 141–43, 150
    unnecessary choice 142
    'Yes/ No' 142
    see also answers
quick speaking 91–92, 101

Radio 5 Live 70, 147–48
Rawl, Lawrence 170–71, 174, 176,
    181, 185
Reagan, Ronald 37, 113–14,
    165–66
'really?' moments 52–53, 58
reciprocation 155, 160
recorded broadcast (TV) interviews 46,
    80–82, 83, 176
reflecting sympathy 175–76
reflective glance down 87
Regan, Tom 157–58, 160, 162, 163
relevance 6
remembering messages 54–58
repeating negatives 143
repetition 139, 150
    key messages 138–40
    see also repeating negatives
Research in Motion (RIM) 75, 134–37
responses
    cautious 72
    'What I can say is' 142–43
retail industry 37
reverse (opposite) opinion 151–52
risks 62
Roosevelt, Franklin D 47

Ruddock, Philip 78–79, 82
Rush Limbaugh Show 2
Russia 166
Russo, Isabel 66–67

Sackur, Stephen 156–57
ScaffMag 6
sceptical audiences 151–68
script, corporate 20
scripted messages 20
Sedgwick, Duncan 69–70
self-explanatory messages 37
self-mockery 118
self-protection 171, 172
sensitive information 19–20, 26
Serbia 166
set, dressing the 23
seven word messages 34
shaking head 160–61
Shaw, Bernard 76
short bridges of empathy 153–54
simplicity 57–58
simulated interviews 24
    see also practice interviews
sincerity 104–05, 124, 159
sit-down interviews 89–90
Sky News 70
Skype interviews 87
slow speaking 92
smiling 93, 101, 160
Smith, Chloe 132–33
smoking messages 129–30
'so what' test 31–36
social media 48, 195–96, 198
    see also Twitter
Solzhenitsyn, Alexander 80
soundbites 47–48, 113
space, use of 89
speaking too quickly 91–92, 101
specialist terminology 110–12
spectrum of opinion 151–52
Sperry, Roger 45
spokespersons 11, 19, 21–22, 23–24
stand-up interviews 88–89
standing up 90
S.T.A.R. (Something They'll Always
    Remember) moments 52–53
statements 8–9, 174, 188
stopping talking 122
stories (storytelling) 5, 8, 12, 31, 38, *42*, 50
strength 119, 182
stress-testing messages 24
style 12
sub-messages 29, 30, 31
sub-Saharan Africa 92

subject matter 12
summaries, negative 142
supercharged messages 34
sympathy 172–78, 182–83, 190
    words 180

talking, stopping 122
target (niche) audiences 110–12
technology
    messages 30–31, 111, 184
    mobile 43
temper control 61–84
10 word messages 33–36, 46, 53, 58
tension 66
terminology
    legal 110–11
    specialist 110–12
TF1 111
thank you notes 197
Thatcher, Margaret *47, 48*
'There were three of us in this marriage'
    35, 37
This Morning 118–19
Thomas, Adrienne 67–68
Thompson, Jeremy 72–74
thought shaping 91–92
three key messages 29–45
thumb in mouth voice exercise 66
Today Programme 6–7, 69–70, 115–16
tongue-tied sensation 65
tongue twisters 66
top-line messages 34–35, 44–45, 49, 56
    see also key messages
Total Confidence (Davies) 64
tourism 38–39, 43
training 24–26
tree conservation 39
trust 2, 10, 56, 85
Tunbridge Wells Courier 2
Tutu, Bishop Desmond 92
TV
    high-definition 101
    interviews 22–23, 26, 56, 98, 99–101, 176
20 second message sandwich 47–48
'2012 is going to be the Twitter election' 35
Twitter *35*, 196, 197
    tweets 195

UK 166
unattributable information 149
Uncommon Help 64
unfair questions 76–77, 141–43, 150
university messages 30, 131
unnecessary choice questions 142
US 166

ValuJet disaster (1996) 177–78
verbosity 122
video interviews 56
videos 196
Vine, Jeremy 106
vocal modulation 94, 101
voice 85–86, 90–92, 94–99, 101,
        103–25, 194
    exercises 65–67, 83
von Rickenbach, Josef H 186–88

Walker, Malcolm 123
Walsh, Willie 184–85, 189
Ward, Peter 80–82
warmth 103, 105–07, 110, 119,
        182, 183
Washington Post 78–79, 82

websites 51, 64
'What I can say is' response 142–43
WHDH-TV 16–17
Winfrey, Oprah 64
W.I.S.E. tone 103–07, 119, 124, 194
    see also empathy; enthusiasm;
        intelligent voice tone; sincerity;
        warmth
word-hugs 156
words 20, 56
    filler 94–98, 101
    sympathy 175–76, 180, 190

yawning voice exercises 66
'yes' questions 142

Zardari, Asif Ali 22